Don't Shop M

Edition 1

2022

Thank you to the poor souls I've worked with, I've served and have managed. You have all suffered in some way, but I hope that now you can see the poor hollow husk of a man that is left, you can sleep easy knowing things didn't work out for me in the end.

richscarrwriter@gmail.com

DON'T SHOP ME NOW

BY

RICH SCARR

After 25 years on the shop floor in retail, here are some of the things I've learned that will help you both work in a shop and shop in a shop whilst they still exist.

PROLOGUE

Cashier number 4 please!

Thank you for choosing to visit our retail outlet today.

Do you have your loyalty card? No, that's your account card, no that's your Nectar card…and that's your Clubpoints. No matter! It's just if you had your loyalty card you could get to hear from Rich here. He does look a bit second hand doesn't he? We did have people like that a long time ago didn't we? But no, they call it "vintage" now. It's not bags under his eyes, that's "patina". Anyway, if you sign up for your loyalty card today he will give you unfettered access to his nearly 30 years in retail and tell you how to get the most out of being on both sides of the counter and how the British high street is really run. What? No, its not as dry as it sounds, its quite funny actually and he frames it all around a day in the life of a shop so it doesn't seem to drag which is a bonus. What did you say? You think you've found your card? Oh lovely. Let's see now...no that's for Lidl, I'll be honest I didn't even know they did them.

CHAPTER 1

OPENING UP

The morning alarm on my phone goes off. The alarm tone on my iPhone is a result of the kind of audio dissection that sits between the surface seriousness of a BBC 4 Friday music doc and the chin stroking chat of late night Radio 6. It needs to be both annoying and shrill enough to smash through my natural ambivalence to external noise whilst I'm sleeping but also pleasant enough to not put me in the kind of mood to have me looking through Duck Duck Go results (is that what we have to use now?) for signifiers of sociopathy. For those interested I settled on "Radar" which, now I think about it, is probably the default setting.

I sit up on the edge of the bed and wait for my brain to reboot. Each morning feels a little bit like being born, but if birth was really tedious. It feels like a really unnecessary procedure, what was wrong with just leaving things how they were, all cosy and, warm and utterly unreal? But no, that's not for us. There is far too much "backing Britain and getting on with *it* to be done and so we must up and out into the sharp grey knife of the day. I throw on a t-shirt and shorts and go downstairs. Nobody wants to hear about ablutions so let's just take those for granted and move onto breakfast. I fill the kettle and whilst it's boiling I stand, dead eyed and vacant faced, leaning against the kitchen worktop pondering what I can face eating. I have the same mental dialogue every morning with the same conclusion.

"I should have that granola with some almond milk. Maybe have a green tea with it. I really need a coffee to feel a bit more lively. Did you know coffee doesn't wake you up, the caffeine just inhibits the receptors that deal with the feelings of fatigue. Yes, yes I did know that. I can't face crunching nuts and seeds at this time in a morning. Hot buttered toast and a big mug of fatigue inhibitor will do the trick." And as a side dish, two anti depressants, vitamin D and something that may or may not improve "gut health". I have only the vaguest inkling of what constitutes gut health but when you reach middle age and things just stop working properly then anything is worth a bash (apart from cod liver oil which was a necessity but is now a folly, although may be a necessity again next week).

Ageing is the most well trod path we have as a species and yet it comes as a surprise to most individuals when it happens. I am "late forties/ early fifties" according to those scrolling age sectors in online forms, into a period where you describe your age in eras rather than specifics.

You've lived so long that individual annual increments are a bit pointless to state unless you're applying for a loan or a passport. Even in the times of face mask wearing in the supermarket no assistant in their right mind is going to ask you for ID when you scan those three bottles of Sainsbury's House Red at the self checkout (should have bought a box). No, no matter how much you treat your body like a temple nobody is going to mistake a 40 something for under 21. We are always going to have a "lived in" aura. Just like animals can detect fresh from partially decaying meat so the checkout assistant knows when to swipe their card over the terminal and press "obviously over 21" without giving you a second glance. No, being 21 is like that moment when you first peel off that thin layer of cellophane from the screen of your phone when you've just unboxed it, all pristine, fully physically formed and full of potential and whether you're the kind of person that pops it into a protective case with a screen

4

cover or lobs it straight into their pocket and leaves it rattling round in the car cupholder, eventually it looks a bit dated and the software won't understand new apps. The only difference is nobody artificially slows your heart down so you buy another one every two years.

Just going back a little, "treating your body like a temple" is the exact opposite of its intended meaning. Temples look like shit, they're old, odd shaped, difficult to keep at a decent temperature and every other year everyone has to rally round to raise enough spare change to stop the rain pissing in on the congregation. It should be used to describe someone who's barely keeping things together -

 "Look at that poor fucker, he's never been the same since his wife left him. Once she got her own flat in town he started treating his body like a temple, it's so sad".

I'm going to use a tenuous car metaphor for my own physical state. It is an admittedly lazy approach and I'm sure it's been done before but I can't be bothered to think of something more intellectual and I've got other things to do in a bit.

Much like my car I was formally a sporty number, not so much a Mclaren, think more hot-hatch, Mini Cooper S let's say. Now I've put some miles on and the regular servicing has got a little lax, a few things have started to need attention. When you aren't flush with cash you tend to just ignore the advisories on the MoT and it's the same with me. The odd noticeable ache, twinge, lessening of hearing/eyesight, unusual toilet are all noted but put off until the mechanic/doctor says that they'll need to be addressed. The big difference I've noticed is when I go to my mechanic and he says "We'll have to replace both rear shocks or it will be undriveable. I've ordered you the two new ones and I can pop them in on Wednesday" it is a big disappointment (especially as it invariably happens when I've just saved some money for spunking away on something useless but enjoyable) but it comes nowhere near to the disappointment of going to the doctors to be told that the thing that's gone wrong with you is just natural wear and tear.

"Yeah, it's the ligaments in your knee"

"Right, so, what do we do about that. Is it a physio job or will it need surgery"

"NHS doesn't do surgery for that kind of thing. Could go private, pricey though, have you got health insurance?"

"No. I always thought it was too expensive, plus a bit pessimistic. Physio then?"

"Yep. I can't guarantee it will work of course. The list is 6 months at the minute but you can pay and get in earlier, just let me have a quick look...here we are, £120"

"For the course of treatment?"

"Per session I'm afraid"

"How many sessions?"

"Depends. Depends on how you react to the treatment and how they think you're progressing"

"So the people I'm paying £120 an hour to get to decide when its best that I stop paying them £120 an hour?

"That's about the size of it"

"What happens if it gets chronic and I can't use it anymore?"

"We'll pop you in for surgery then. Have you got an active job?"

"Are there many scenarios where you don't need knees?"

"A lot of people lead very productive lives without them."

"I'm sorry, I thought I came in here to sort out a pain in my leg not to apply for funding for the Paralympics. Can't you give me anything for it now?"

"I can prescribe some anti-inflammatories. Take away the swelling."

"Will that help?"

"Might. Swelling causes a lot of everyday pain."

"Well that's saved me a search on WebMD"

"You work at that shop don't you? I'm after a new washing machine. I want one of those nice German ones but they're a bit expensive aren't they? Have you got any offers on?"

"We tend not to have offers on the good stuff that's worth the money. I suppose I could sort you out with an ex-display model. There'll be a sales consultation fee. £120 an hour. Little private medical joke there. No? Pop in on Thursday and ask for me, I'll sort you out"

"Great. Do they take away the old machine?"

"Yes."

"Do they install the new one and take the boxes away? I've not got a big bin you see and I'm not driving all the way to the tip."

"Not all that way to the tip like a commoner? Yes they'll do all that for £50. If you make them a brew and they'll give your prostate a check as well. Don't use your best mugs though."

"Ha! Yes! See you Thursday."

You'll have gathered from that that I both work in a shop and am a bit of a git. I've found over the years that not only aren't the two things exclusive but they are almost a prerequisite for both mentally surviving in retail and for being quite good at it. An entirely unnecessary amount of the shopping process revolves around people trying to take the piss.

This piss taking might involve colleagues -

"I know you've done the last month of lates and weekends and I've just come back from holiday, but my sisters friend has just come back from New Zealand and she wants to take us out for a meal so could you do my weekend? I'll be in too much of a state on Sunday to come in and I want to get my haircut on Saturday before we go out?" - Piss take.

"Dave was supposed to put the Sale tickets out last night but he had to leave early because his baby had trapped wind. Can you come in early and do them?" - Piss take.

For variety it can involve delivery people or contractors -

"That floor needs a special drill. Nobody told us it needs a special drill. We've not brought the special drill."

"Can you not get the special drill now? I've come in for this night shift especially"

"Nah mate. Special drill's in Chelmsford. By the time we got there and back it would be morning. Besides they're shut. We can maybe do it next Thursday, possibly" - Piss take. Special drill piss take, one of the worst of the piss takes.

Sometimes customers like to have a bash to see how it feels in their mouths -

"Hi, can I get a refund on this?"

"Sure, have you got your receipt?"

"I haven't no, I did buy it here though."

"Have you got any proof of purchase?"

"No."

"Anything? Bank statement? Did you pay for it with your store card or maybe use your loyalty card? We could look it up on the system then. Two minute job."

"No, I paid cash. Look, I did buy it from here. Can't you look on the cameras or something."

"I'm sorry no we can't and I'm afraid it would only show you in the shop."

"But I bought it here! Where else would I have bought it?"

"Well it is an Apple Watch so you could theoretically have purchased it in a variety of outlets. We need the receipt so we know how much to refund you because without the price details from when you say you bought it we may give you less than you should get if there's a sale on at the moment. Plus, theoretically, someone could just pick something up from the shelves and bring it to the till and ask for a refund if we didn't ask for proof of purchase."

"Are you accusing me!   I'd like to see the store manager right now!" - Big fat customer piss take, plus - as if the Manager gives a shit.

Being a git helps to deal with the annoyance at being asked to take someones piss, the feeling that they've specially selected you as a suitable piss recipient and in reversing their particular yellow hued stream right back at them. The aim is to be both bone dry and sweet smelling at the end of each and every day if you've achieved this give yourself a pat on the back or preferably a vodka and tonic.

One of the things I realised on my road to git-dom was that we can all do well to remember to learn from others. Just think about that person at work who can be a bit of an arse on occasion but at the same time doesn't have to deal with half of the annoyances in a normal work day that you do, that seems like a pretty good deal doesn't it? The other thing you will quickly realise is that you don't need to use this super power very often at all before the seed is planted in peoples minds that you may well be a bit of a shit if they ask you to cover a shift/deal with that customer/work a 12 hour shift because Dan has rung in sick again, and they slowly stop asking you. Never underestimate just how much people will be inclined to take the path of least resistance.

No, all it takes is a few well timed moments of mild arse like behaviour and you are almost there. Don't get me wrong, I am an inherently decent person so this doesn't come without emotional struggle, but at the same time that's a good thing. It's those freaks for who this comes to them purely instinctively that you need to steer clear of. They aren't being a bit of an arse for the long term benefits, these people are what we refer to as "Pricks" and sometimes "Absolute Pricks" and while we can always learn something from them, nobody should want to be one, even if it means you end up as Chairperson of the company. As the old saying goes, not all pricks are company chairmen but all company chairmen are pricks.

Once you have established your reputation for potential gittery you will find that work suddenly becomes that bit easier. You will find the inane questions will reduce to a minimum, requests to cover other peoples tardiness drift away and when you do get asked to do a shit job it will be done with such trepidation and reluctance that you will be treated like a charity raising war hero for complying without remark. I like to imagine that this must be a little bit how people who are naturally attractive drift through their day, or perhaps its more apposite to think of it as being like someone who was a bit of a pig/moose throughout school before turning into a Hull/ Leeds level Ryan Reynolds/Charlize Theron.

That way you see both sides of the fence and appreciate the one you're on.

Having firmly established my reputation I have unashamedly gilded the lily, I have installed the gold toilet, I have worn my Gucci sneakers to Aldi, if you will, by developing the "face". The face is one of those skills, a bit how I imagine being fluently bilingual through learning (and not cheating by having multi cultural parents) must feel. A lot of time and ball ache to get there but when you do it becomes second nature and something that you can slip in and out of without thinking.

Many peoples "Faces" are different for achieving a variety of effects and I can only speak knowledgeably about mine. Now I must admit I have a naturally resting face that gives the signal "I think you're all morons spouting endless shit." This isn't self diagnosis, this has come from many, many years of feedback from a wide spectrum of people. Film makers across the world would kill for the kind of accurate, unfettered verbal feedback and subsequent data I have received when they are test screening. This feedback is, of course, invaluable. It's no use having that face naturally and not knowing how it can be utilised. I'm happy with my face-message. I'm not sure if I would have chosen it but it suits me. It sends a subliminal message to customers that suggests "I'm not sure exactly why but I think I'll find someone else to ask about this blender" and for that I'll always be glad.

Once I had realised my face-state I developed subtle facial muscles, much in the style, I imagine, of certain actors who always seem to end up with the close ups in films.

"Such amazing acting, he seems to convey so much with just the raise of an eyebrow" well yeah, it's piss easy to do that when the lens is resting on your nose for 5 minutes and there's no distractions. Try conveying that in a department store in Liverpool on a Friday afternoon and then I'll start sitting up, Bobby De Niro (actually he's a bad example. I'm sure he has some awful dark reason for the scripts he's chosen recently but overall, ignoring them, I think it's fair to say he is a very competent performer).

No, my subtle nuances convey -

Disinterest - (with sub headings of outright contempt for even suggesting whatever it is you're saying).

Emotional fatigue - from whatever low intellect drivel you deign to inflict on me with an unstoppable realisation that you are, without doubt or question, a fucking moron.

The "Roman Emperor" - This one emits the feeling that I am physically in your presence but I am so far above and removed from it that I might as well not be in the same building. That it's all bit of a waste getting me involved in something so low level.   Like asking Professor Brian Cox whether you're in a hard or soft water region.

These are all applied with use and non use of facial muscles.   I can't go into the details right now [emotional fatigue face] but suffice to say it takes a great deal of practice, but (and I cannot stress this enough) it is worth it.   You never know when it will need to be deployed. As a side effect, which must have come naturally but is useful, I have a distinct "thinking" face.   Most people have a thinking face. That one when your brain is so consumed with thought that it uses it's resources on whatever computations it needs to process that it puts the "what am I doing with my facial expressions" RAM to better use. For some poor unfortunates their thinking faces drop into a sort of gormless, fish-feeding coma like state, as if they suddenly can't marry the colours and shapes dichotomy together enough to put that red wooden cube in the right hole. I am blessed with a face that when my brains resources start to run at 90% my face falls into the kind of expression that apparently says to those around me "talk or don't talk, I'm not listening. I have the distinct feeling only I can come up the answer." Sadly this is just a natural by product of my facial muscle relaxation as I am genuinely just thinking about how to fix the problem. Still, I'd rather that than the fish-feeding face (it must be noted that many social media influencers are making a cracking living holding this face to camera in a variety of Missguided/Pretty Little Thing outfits and fair play to them, I would if I could).

I apologise, where were we? Ah yes, we're on our way to the shop. It is also sometimes referred to as a "store" or "outlet" or "branch" but it's not, it's a shop. People who refer to it as something other than that are just trying to elevate it to sounding like somewhere serious business people or the middle class might deign to visit on occasion or not feel ashamed of saying where they work.

"I do some work for a store in the centre" does I'll admit sound more like you're popping in to Nike HQ to do consultancy work after your hot yoga session rather than covering the afternoon till shift in The Works but really saying that instead of "I work in that books and stationery shop in town" is just pandering to other peoples imaginary judgement. When I ask what people do I'm not looking for an answer so that I can put you in a mental league list standing of what I deem impressive jobs, I'm asking because your answer prompts me what to say in our next bit of conversation. That's why it's "what do you do?" Not "what do you do for a job?", what you do leaves it open to what your passion is, what your hobby is and I like to think most people who aren't cripplingly insecure about their own social standing are asking that for the same reason so the next time someone asks go with "artist", "gardener", "gymnast", it will make for a more interesting chat. Of course this doesn't work in a job interview situation, although I would say, after having experience from both sides of the desk, you can say any old shit. Nobody will follow up on it and check until it's too late and by then you'll have passed your probationary period and learned how to do formulas in excel from YouTube.

Edit: I found it was all very well me getting all "Street Preacher" about not using other words for "shop" before I decided to write a book where on many, many occasions I have to find another word for "shop" to stop it getting repetitive. Rest assured shop worker me has given writer me a bit of a talking to.

I'm blessed in my commute and never take it for granted. Over the years I have had to take the bus, the train, walk and drive for hours at the start and end of each day for different jobs and it really makes a difference to your whole day. For a recent job I had to leave at 5.00am, drive in a combination of motorway and inner city traffic, search for the least extortionate parking opportunity before a half hour walk through the zombie morning promenaders to arrive at work two hours after I'd left the house. This never left me bursting with excitement about what opportunities the day may hold or what I could achieve in my work time. At best I was numb and tired and, after a year of mid day comfort eating, fat. I'm in no way saying I had the worst of commutes, I wasn't hanging off a train on my way to sort through a tip for tradeable plastic.

It's just to point out that the way your colleagues behave, the way your customers interact with you first thing in the morning may be because they've just had to pay £20 to a toothless bloke dressed in shorts and a high vis waistcoat that's clearly been rescued from a bin just to park their car on some wasteland that's £5 cheaper than the nicely lit council one down the road.

My commute is relative bliss and after all the other shit commutes I've had over the years I positively revel in it. Some days it's a singing day, some it's time to listen to the rest of that podcast I started at breakfast, occasionally it's "Today" on Radio 4 (for when I'm feeling particularly emotionally strong and stoic and can handle the vivid hellscape they reveal outside). Sometimes I make up songs or jingles about the local company on the van in front of me on the road and end up wondering how Ed Sheeran has ended up where he is. Sometimes I'll do traffic reports in an accent (American, Geordie,

Australian, I'm not that adventurous) and on occasion I'll repeat what the people on the radio say in the voice of David Bowie and then try and shake that off before I arrive at work sounding like I've popped in for a session with Brian Eno. My favourite commutes are when I take the motorbike in on an early morning and the dew is rising from the fields and the sky is a pink, orange and violet. The beauty and wonder of this is balanced by my groans in the locker room as I try and get out of my bike gear as if I've just crawled back into the lunar lander after a moon potter.

And then we are there. At the shop. What customers probably don't think about, and quite rightly, is what goes into getting everything ready for them. Unloading the lorries and vans of goods, getting it all on the shelves, the pricing, the cleaning and most importantly the moaning about the people who were in the night before who were too fucking lazy to tidy up ready for you coming in in the morning and doing the real work.   In large shops and department stores there are specialist teams responsible for specific tasks such as a loading bay team who make sure all the stock is unloaded and signed in and excess stock is loaded to be taken away, merchandise teams who make sure the shelves are filled and the products are ticketed, perhaps a finance/shop support team who make sure the tills are filled and emptied and the systems are all running how they should.   There might be a Visual team who dress the windows, put on promotions and deal with displays, mannequin styling etc and on top of all that there will be managers/supervisors who make sure all this is being completed and that's before the sales team/assistants come in to serve you and man the floor all watched over by security/loss prevention. A whole host of different skills and abilities, a vast amount of experience and training to know exactly what needs doing, when and by whom. All joined by one piece of knowledge, one conviction, one absolute certainty and that is that they are all convinced that the whole operation would fall apart if they weren't there and that a significant proportion of the others they work with are a) Lazy b) Shit or c) Both.

Morning pre opening is often punctuated by minor bullet point events. Things such as what radio station is on in the shop when you're shelf filling, what email has some sly fucker sent you 10 minutes after you left yesterday with a list of shit to do in the morning, who has rung in sick again and perhaps most important of all, when are the engineers coming in to fix the vending machine in the staff canteen ("This is a fucking outrage! Every morning this is! No coffee in a morning! If this was France we'd have burnt some sheep by now! It's one thing they do get right!").

And so dear readers it is time for us to open the front doors, when we can find the key ("Why did they put it there last night? He's such a dick. When are they going to fix this shutter properly, they were only here last Wednesday? Christ these new shoes are crippling me already. "Good morning! It's what sorry?...a return? Yes any till." Fuck me, starting off with a refund").

CHAPTER 2

CONTACTLESS

And now we arrive at the time when we must allow entry to the great unwashed, although in the case of the last shop I worked in it was more of a case of the fragrant or "too posh to wash". This also coincides with the teams who have been in early prepping the shop for customers starting to think about what to eat on their break or how much they want a fag/vape. Both good excuses to get off the shop floor. If you haven't worked in a shop or catering it may come as a surprise to you that there is a sizeable population of the workforce who don't want to have anything to do with customers. This sounds odd, I mean without customers there wouldn't be jobs in shops but I like to think about it this way - without sickness, injury and death there wouldn't be jobs in hospitals either but we wouldn't be complaining about it. Do you think that M.P.'s like their constituents? Do you think they like door knocking for support or holding surgeries for a queue of the ill informed? No, of course they don't. They like getting shit done, creating a positive legacy, claiming expenses on packets of crisps and banging randoms at conferences.

CUSTOMER TIP

The perfect time to shop is normally an hour after the opening time. Of course the shop is officially open at 9am but the staff probably aren't mentally awake yet or they haven't finished telling Nick about how that definitely wasn't a penalty last night and that it's one rule for the top clubs and another for the rest and why can they get VAR right in big tournaments but not in the Prem and it's ridiculous when they've got all that money and just when he's about to make this really good point about the fans taking 51% ownership in clubs and taking the power back (a point he would have made last night on TalkSport if he hadn't have been driving his youngest, Kyle, to karate) you stroll up with your bag for life from another shop asking if he can help you find a kettle for someone with weak wrists, a request which is of course met with all the enthusiasm of a death row inmate. No, unless you know exactly what you want, where it is and that it's on the shelf waiting I would recommend leaving it an hour. Plus the staffing levels first thing are always shit so it's better to wait until a nice part-timer starts at 10 because she knows exactly what you mean because Doris down the road was after a kettle just like that, not for home, for the caravan. They don't do that one she has at home any more, which is a shame but that's how things are these days isn't it?

As an added bonus the shop is looking as good as it's going to get that day and all the stock they have will be out.

I like things to look good and I'm fortunate enough that that is also the aim of my job. I like things to be arranged and positioned in a carefully considered way so they are attractive and interesting to you. It doesn't have to be interesting to me, I'm not the customer. I get paid to make you want the product. Actually that's not really true. That's something I tell myself on a daily basis to get me through the hours of work. What businesses pay me for is to implement someone in head offices idea of what customers want, which is usually so nondescript that they might as well have sent a blank PDF or they've been working from a list of products the buyers gave them late on Thursday with a Friday deadline and then you find out that you don't have any of the products (they are always either on a boat or have just recently fallen off a boater or are in the process of being loaded onto a boat which will then fall over).

I will come across as unreasonably negative about the people who work in head offices and that is because they are usually, barring a few small exceptions, a bit shit, sometimes total shit. When I first started working in retail I thought that Head Office was some kind of mix of Bletchley Park and the Parisian Left Bank in the 1920's, all great minds and creativity that achieved their lofty positions from working their way through the ranks, earning their place in the retail Premier League through hard work, wit, invention and proven results. You will find some of these people in the office, they are usually sat looking wistfully out of the window or outside having a fag telling a fellow co-smoker how they aren't going to "do another fucking Christmas here". When you call Head Office to solve a problem you will often find yourself conversing with Jessica/Jamie who have never sold anything (apart from that jacket that they loved from that little boutique that's not there any more that got a cigarette burn in the arm that night stood outside Simmons in Camden. Far too nice to throw away, pop it on eBay for £250, it did cost £300 after all) but they did study Modern History and Politics and didn't ring in sick once while they were interning which now somehow inexplicably leaves them qualified as the best person to head up merchandising for menswear. Like if Scunthorpe United got dropped into the Champions League Semi Finals every year because they were always the first to get their round in after work.

Spend any amount of time in Head Office and you will quickly realise that each department, just like the shops, thinks that all the other departments are full of lazy morons. The individuals they do like are often poached to work in their departments. Working in a close proximity for most of your waking hours means that it can be tempting to just try and surround yourself with people who are pleasant to get on with regardless of the merits of their abilities, which is completely understandable but not much help when you've been sent 200 denim jackets but they're all extra small. As a side note this issue of single sizes popped into my head because I've come across it a lot in Primark. The number of times I've come across racks of product only to find they're all the same size. I wonder if they have some unusual arrangement with their factories to get the products cheap? "We can make those red plaid shirts for 50p a unit but we'll need to make all the small ones first, then all the mediums, then larges and XL's.

We'll send them over as we've made each size and hopefully the boat won't fall over this time."

Something that everyone in Head Office has in common is that they don't like leaving there to have to visit a shop in their chain. It's only when they have to leave the London bubble (it's usually London, unless it's a business created by a "Northerner made good" who is "not going to pay those prices for an office") that they realise what they have in their normal office environment. The general view from head office workers of the worker drones in shops is that they just don't get it. They don't understand the complexities of working at the top like they do, the budgets, the timelines, the deadlines, buying the right product, margins, not having enough time to nip out to Itsu *and* return that top to All Saints. They simply just don't get it, it's probably something to do with the air from the pit or the mill affecting them when they are young.

An unfortunate byproduct of not visiting shops on a semi regular basis is that when they do they face a barrage of questions and pent up frustrations from the shop workers and often these questions are aimed at Head Office in general as an entity.

"Why didn't we get any of the local schools ties in to sell this year?"

"We sold loads of those galvanised flower vases last year and this year you didn't send us any. It's not like we didn't do them, Janice was in Norwich visiting her sister and she said they had loads in there"

"That new coffee you got us for the cafe tastes like it's burnt, is it supposed to be like that? Is it a London thing?"

"I'm sorry I don't know, I just buy the towels. Sometimes the toilet seats if Harriet is pushed for time"

There will also be the young and fresh faced who will be eager to ingratiate themselves with the metropolitan demi-god in the hopes they will be talent spotted and whisked off to the capital for a life of press shows and sharing a few lines of coke that smells like kitchen spray with a shoe designer from Brazil, or maybe Argentina, one of them anyway. The reality being they might get in on a role (because it was a particularly bad intern year) only to find out that the starting salary assumes that you are from London and are living rent free with your parents and are walking to work or that you are happy living in that two bedroom shared house with eight other people that's only an hours commute away from the nearest tube station.

CUSTOMER TIP

This is a tricky one to time right but if you visit a shop and they are moving things, painting, looking hurried and distracted then it will probably be because they are "expecting a visit". This visit will not be from royalty, the local MP or even the winners of Love Island 2019, it will be from a Regional Manager/Head of Sales for the North/Sales Director. The shop manager will then make every effort possible for the shop to look as good as possible and run to perfection for that day. If you ask a member of staff "you look busy, are you expecting a visit?" And they reply with a weary look "yes, tomorrow" leave the shop and come back the next day. There you will find previously unseen numbers of staff on departments. Normally two on white goods? How about eight today). Normally greeted with indifference? Well today we have someone who doesn't really know why they are there but will welcome you at the entrance to say "Good morning!" whilst avoiding eye contact and looking uncomfortable. Not only will Nick help you find a weak wrist kettle but he'll give you a demonstration of the top three and Sarah will carry it to your car. The service levels will have you feeling like Mary Portas has arranged an exclusive after hours personal shopping trip just for you.

From a customers point of view they should advertise these days rather than some of the other meaningless promotions. Fuck Mother's Day off and put out ads promoting an actual pleasant shopping day.

Of course none of this is for you, it's not for the shop or the shop workers. It's for the Shop Manager, the assistant manager and the various department managers and supervisors.

It's the chance to show the VIP visitor what they can do in the hopes that they can get that promotion and get the hell out of there, maybe get that flagship store and that new 5 series that Clarkson was raving about. For the Assistant Manager etc its a chance to get on the Visitors radar and hopefully they'll all move up one, maybe get the Shop Managers Audi A3 if he won't be needing it. This charade is played out by all concerned, the Manager pretends the shop always looks like this, that they're really maximising it's potential. The Visitor pretends they don't know it doesn't and the other managers pretend that they always know the figures for their department and they haven't spent the previous night revising them or being coached on what to say. But still, they did say good morning and carried your kettle to the car, which is something, even if it did mean the shop will be about two grand over on payroll for that month for getting every student on the books in to work on a Wednesday.

Retail isn't complicated, shops aren't complicated. Thousands of people with no retail experience have made successful businesses just by selling something to a customer for more money than it cost them to sell it. Buy it for £10, advertise it for £5, post it for £2, sell it for £25. Simple.

The complicated bit isn't what you do, it's what you stop doing. You get complacent, stop thinking about the customers that you have and what they will want, stop looking for new customers and how to broaden your appeal. You stop always thinking about what it's like for people to shop with you (even though you'll find people in managerial positions love to talk about the "customer experience"). You stop surrounding yourself with people who are passionate about the product and the act of shopping. You stop talking to the very people who are selling your products, who interact with your customers everyday, to see what they think and what people are saying to them about their needs. They lose touch, lose the focus that made the business a success in the first place. How many times have you walked into a shop that you previously enjoyed visiting and walked out thinking that they'd really lost their way and maybe you will try online next time? It's because they've become complacent, lazy. Large businesses fall every year because of it and it's such a simple thing to prevent, not easy but simple. It requires effort, effort to surround yourself with the right people, create the right atmosphere and keep on doing it very day, month, year and if you can't be arsed why would your customers?

CHAPTER 3

BAG FOR LIFE

I love shopping.

I absolutely fucking love it. I completely understand why people don't like it, hate it even. I feel like that about lots of things, sorting out my financial future, finding someone to fix the guttering, Eastenders. I also get that if you're skint and shopping comprises of a trip to the food bank or that you're pushed for time because you're trying to find a vaccine for a global pandemic going out to try on a pair of New Balance isn't going to be high on the "fun must do" list so lets focus on the mean for now.

My perfect shopping experience would be in Manhattan. Just like shopping I love Manhattan. New York is a bloody big place and I haven't been to much of it so I'll be specific in where I like. I love so much about it, the atmosphere, the film set surroundings, the buzz of things happening and people making them happen, the architecture, the scale, the people but most of all I love the shopping. It's all the things I love about the shopping experience but multiplied.

Walking past the stores with stalls outside groaning under the weight of fruit, vegetables and flowers to get to a restaurant that's open for breakfast and sit by the window eating eggs and drinking coffee while watching commuters in cool shades and awful coats go by to work and guessing what they do for a living. Marvelling at how shit the driving is before getting a refill and working out where we are going to go that day.

I'm lucky enough to be married to someone who shares the same passion for this experience so we will sit and work out the shops that are on our must see list for that day and plan the order and the route we will take. This sounds like a design for the opposite of spontaneous fun but we walk everywhere when we're there (apart from a cab home) so it's just so we aren't walking for hours in the wrong direction. I like the walk to all the various places, taking in the buildings, the people's half heard conversations, discovering shops I haven't seen before, finding products that are new to you, that feeling of what the shop is all about. The thing to remember is that all these places exist for you. They are there just for you to go in and let them show you things they think you might like and leave happy and wanting to come back one day, what is there to not like about that? At some point we will stop for brunch and a couple of bloody Mary's in Soho, more people-watching and listening before setting off for another wander. High end shops like Chanel, Prada, Louis Vuitton are all good to go in as you get to see some really great design in terms of the shop fixtures and decor as well as getting to see exactly why a pair of trousers could cost $650, plus the staff have always been great in them (my experience is not universal). It's not just about high end shops, there are great independents and discount retailers that have made an effort to make the experience enjoyable as well. Fish's Eddy is a brilliant independent stocking home wares and clearly shows the passion in the product from its owners in the what they select, the fixtures and displays and how it's all laid out. Don't get me wrong, there are a lot of shit shops with poor service, drab displays, poor products but I don't go to them in the same way that I don't sit all the way through a terrible film on Netflix, although if it is really bad I will, it makes for a good topic of conversation if nothing else. I used to love visiting Macy's, it was a big old American timewarp of a department store and, outside of the bar downstairs (which has now sadly gone), the service was utter shit. They showed such utter disinterest and disdain it drifted into the comedic. When they talked to you without looking at you ("sign here" whilst looking at the front door) before throwing your bag at you and serving the next person while you are still there you would end up pausing, waiting to hear the laugh track and have George Costanza shout "Hey! Can you see me? Am I invisible? Do I need a doctor or a scientist for invisibility, I've never dealt with this before? Unbelievable." We actually used to look forward to going to the till to see how bad it would be.

We plan the store we will probably spend the most in as the last stop (mini customer tip: remember your bag logistics) and then get a cab back to the hotel, then food, late night cocktails and a chat with the barman before sleep and doing it all again the next day. Of course since austerity became the new national sport I've had to make do with imagining the Trafford Centre is on par with Fifth Avenue but I think the point still stands.

I see shops as a bunch of physical ideas that people want to share and though the experience does rely on you buying into it to a certain extent they aren't asking you to dress up and role play (well, some shops do but that's a different chapter). I understand it's not for everyone, some people would rather go to the match and for those people I would say just think about what makes that an enjoyable experience? Isn't part of it the trip down there and a pint on the way? Seeing all the different characters walking in, betting on whether that bloke who's bought five drinks will make it back to his seat without spilling them? Listening to the two blokes in front of you explain the tactics they would use having honed them to perfection over the decades they've spent working on the bins. It's the surroundings and the people that make it as we've seen with the soulless closed doors fixtures and for me it's the same with shopping, yes I could never leave the house and just swipe my phone to buy in the same way as I could watch a match at home with no crowds to be seen but it's just not the same.

CUSTOMER TIP

Have you ever been personally shopped? That does sound like I'm asking you to point on the bear where they touched you. I think everyone should have a really good personal shopping at least once in their life (I'm running with the vague suggestive wording). It's arrogant not to. *Going through your entire life thinking that the only person capable of choosing the right clothes for you is yourself. What are your qualifications for it? Where did you learn be such an expert on colour selection, material, fit? More than likely you didn't, you've just been winging it all your life like the rest of us. It's such a rare gift to able to see yourself and a potential different you through someone else's eyes and it's out there for free. Everyone knows that clothes change your personality even if you aren't consciously thinking it at the time, school uniforms, fancy dress, outfit for a wedding, football kit, they all put you in a different frame of mind and having someone else pick out clothes they think could work for does the same thing. In makeover shows, at the end, everyone watching will say "well it was the haircut that made the difference" or "she looks confident now her teeth aren't crooked" which is all valid to a point but how they walk, how they carry themselves and how they see themselves is down to what they are wearing because once they are out of that room that's what people will see. Nobody is looking thinking "she looks newly confident, it must be that fringe" (although they may be thinking "her teeth look great but if I have to drink everything through a straw like I'm paralysed is it worth it?").*

You don't need to be on Channel 4 in the 2000's to get someone else's take on what you might look good in.   There are a lot of personal shoppers in stores that you can book in with for free and, if they are quiet, a lot of fashion stores would be more than happy to try and kit you out with an outfit or two if you ask. You aren't necessarily going to like everything they choose, or even any of it but even if all you do is walk out of there thinking "you know what, I've got great taste, I know more than they do" then that's a nice little confidence booster and something to tell your friends over a drink isn't it (even if they only agree with you until you go to the loo so they can say what they really think about those mum/dad jeans you insist are in)?

When someone else chose clothes they could see me in I was lucky and really liked it all (the fact that they were attractive had nothing/ something to do with it) and even though I didn't stick with that style it did make me a lot more open minded to different things.

Try it, you might like it. This applies to most things with notable exceptions being heroin, meth amphetamine and Pernod. Vile.

Something that probably won't surprise you is the relatively small amount of people who like shops and shopping who are in charge of what shops stock and what they look like. It should surprise you but it won't because you've been in shops that don't make any sense or just don't seem quite right. Maybe the decor doesn't go with the type of product, maybe the order of things is a bit jarring, you've just had to walk through the golf section and kids pushchairs to get to the photo frames. One thing you will find that these Captains of Industry will get right is the location of the till. In these palaces of commerce the till is usually first on the planning list which tells you all you need to know about who is pulling the strings.

Please don't think that I want high street retail to be left in the hands of the creatives, the taste making buyers and those who think a shop is as much a concept as a physical reality (which I think is something I may have said earlier...) Nobody wants that. You only have to look at some of the monstrosities that this group considers the height of creativity on LinkedIn, an empty 4,000 square foot warehouse space save for a vase on a pink acrylic box for you to gaze on as an ambient remix of "Stand By Your Man" plays on a loop. "Brave"? "Edgy"? No, shite.

What you need is the two groups to come together, decide on the goals of each and who is going to do what. The money focussed to say what profit margin is needed, overall turnover, budgets for payroll etc. The creatives and buyers to decide on how best to present these to achieve the financials. When it comes unstuck is when each group decides that they are better informed at doing the other groups work.

Coming from a background of the predominantly creative side of things it never ceased to amaze (and to be honest, annoy) me that a Regional Sales Director felt that they knew more about the styling and placement of mannequins than me despite the fact that at the time I'd been doing it as a job for years, spent my time outside work reading the fashion magazines, seeing what was on the high street, looking at what trends might be coming up from the catwalk, looking at how people were wearing their clothes at events, monitoring what our customers were buying and how they shopped the different areas. But no, apparently I was the one grappling in the dark whilst he a, more often than not, middle aged bloke who spent 5 hours a day in a car, who had no interest in fashion apart from the unit cost and who only visited the shops he was in charge of because he didn't like shopping, especially if The Open golf was on Sky, was striding through the illuminated fields of fashion consciousness.

"Look mate" I would say "How about you wind your fucking neck in about my shit and I won't chip in about the way you budget payroll or that assistant on Clinique you've been seeing on the side, eh?"

Obviously I didn't say that. What the two of us really needed to do is go back to basics, why didn't he like it and what did he think wasn't working? After a good chat you'd usually find out that there was perhaps a line that was particularly profitable that they wanted to push or maybe there was something that they had large amounts of stock of that they could lose money on if those volumes ended up in the sale so then I could re-look at it see how we could best emphasise these to get maximum sales, that way we both use our relative expertise in the most efficient way and he sees the value in what I do and vice versa (to an extent).

Neither side helps their case. The creatives have a tendency to come across as the kind of people who wear dungarees ironically and like the kind of blank page thinking about how to present a sauté pan that may end in a tasteful industrial style fixture that holds the boxed product underneath a metal framed wooden topped table with a display pan and promotional picture but can sometimes start with a thought process involving a winch and pulley system normally seen employed in Cirque du Soleil. If anyone from finance comes across to see how that pan promo that they're hoping will shift 3,000 units is coming along and sees this genesis of thought they will probably think "What is all this wank about? Where's the pan? Why have you got it swinging through the air above a scented candle? I don't know why we can't just leave them on the pallet they arrive from the lorry on." This bit of the design process should be kept firmly in the "initial ideas and inspiration" folder. Again, fix it with a conversation. If the buying team explain that the reason they've bought it is because they are made by local artisans (people who make stuff), the iron is forged in a nearby smith and the wooden handles are made from welsh timber and turned in a joiners across the road from the forge, plus they think they can sell them for three times the cost price after tax. Then the creatives can use this info in making fixtures and posters that talk about the provenance and echo the materials used in the manufacture (get the table tops made in the same wood as the handles etc). Everyone's happy, especially the distributor who's actually buying them from Wish at £1 a pan.

All the best managers I've worked with surround themselves with people who they trust to do the job and carry out the brief. It builds confidence in your teams and boosts morale when they have faith in you to achieve what they want and they'll feel comfortable engaging in a dialogue when they want clarification or assurance that they're heading in the direction the manager wants. Your team loses faith in their own abilities if you're constantly dipping in and trying to do some of the work. They'll also lose enthusiasm for you as a leader if you're not leading, you're doing. They might even start discussing just how much Chanel you're buying for your wife with the amount of time you spend chatting at that counter.

CHAPTER 4

BASKETS & TROLLEYS

CUSTOMER TIP

When is a bargain not a bargain?   When is it time to swap the basket for the trolley?

This is a difficult shopping conundrum. I personally hate sale shopping.   I have a contempt devoid of it's vague sense when I see footage of hundreds of people in a shop on the news, scrabbling round in desperation to get a 60" 4K TV for £200 that was previously £2,000. That TV isn't worth 2 grand, it's not even worth £200.   The business has bought it for, let's say,

£150 inc shipping etc and the manufacturer has managed to put it together for £100. They haven't made the components for it, they've just assembled them from generic components that they have bought from someone else who has got there profit in as well so, broken down into it's actual worth it's probably around £40 of TV that will probably creep over the line in terms of length of use just past the date of the manufacturers warranty. You would be a lot better off buying a smaller TV with less claimed resolution for the same price, better picture for longer.

When it comes to purchases that I have to justify in expense terms to myself I become one of those annoying people who does a lot of research. It doesn't matter what it is, rugs, shower heads, washing machines, irons, lamps, I will looking for reviews. Within those reviews I'm looking not only at the performance and build quality, I'm not made of money, I'm looking at the price and the compromises I'll have to make to get as near to what I want as possible for a price in my budget. Let's take washing machines as an example, the item even my doctor didn't want to buy at full price. I know the best ones are also the most expensive ones. They have the best features, the longest warranties, and having moved dozens of them across shop floors I know they have the best build quality (some Miele's are built with all the weight considerations of a tank designer). I can't justify getting together that amount of money for one even though it's the perfect solution, so I have to look at where I can compromise. I don't need all the washing programmes (two, three max will do for me), I don't need it to automatically feed in the precise amount of detergent and softener from bespoke hoppers in the base (I'm happy just chucking a cap full in the little drawer), I don't need a battle hardened construction (I'd like to die before my washing machine) and as everyone on a budget has to do, I will put up with a shorter warranty and take my chances (which means I've resigned myself to buying another machine in two or three years). So taking all that into consideration I will look for reviews of the ones left. I discard some immediately like the ones from companies with a reputation for passing on products that have a habit of spontaneously combusting, ones that I couldn't live with looking at everyday ("limited edition colour variations in pink, purple, special edition ones emblazoned with the union flag to celebrate 25 years of Brit Pop) and move onto the remainder.

I should say at this point that where you get your reviews from needs to be treated with extreme scepticism and caution. Unscrupulous retailers (unscrupulous is one of those words not used outside of features on scams/rogue tradesmen) will pay for fake positive reviews and there are usually a few poor sites dedicated to reviews at the top of the search pages where they have paid to drag you in to basically farm for clicks for advertising revenue or money from affiliate links. The content on these sometimes been lifted from other articles or is so flimsy that it's useless so it's worth going deeper into the list to find a site you can trust.

Only after all this trawling through information do I then venture into a shop to check it out in person. Speaking of which it's always worth having a chat with someone who works on that area, ask them which ones get returned the most or have the most complaints, they might let you know about a discontinued Miele you can have for the same price, doubtful but maybe.

Another reason I hate sale shopping is because everything looks like shit in the shop. Red tickets everywhere, the pretence of loving the product is given over to just its monetary value.

Ticket: "Look! Look! It's only £5!"

Customer: "What is it?"

Ticket: "It's a golden pineapple!"

Customer: "Not real gold."

Ticket: "No!"

Customer: "What does it do?"

Ticket: "Nothing, it just is!"

Customer: "No thanks"

Ticket: "But it *WAS* £50 and now it's only a fiver!"

Customer: "Will I have to tell everyone that that's why I bought it when they come round to my house and ask why I have a decorative gold pineapple to make the purchase make sense?"

Ticket: "Yes!"

Customer: "Does it come with a box?"

Ticket: "Yes! Slightly damaged!"

Customer: "Fine, I'll take it. That's that nobhead at work's Secret Santa sorted."

I should point out that that conversation was supposed to be between the promotional ticketing in the shop and the customer. It's a bit of an imaginary leap I'll admit and could have done with a better pre-amble but there you are, you probably haven't paid full price for this so you have to take the rough with the smooth.

If you go into a shop towards the end of a sale you'll find the worst mix of products. Nice, new season stock will sit in very small numbers across the aisle from what looks like the content of the skip round the back, all sad, forlorn and unloved. Businesses will persevere for far too long trying to just get anything they can for this old tat rather than bin it and take the loss without taking into account the detrimental effect it has on the sales of the nice new stuff at full price. You can have the best seats in the house for that concert but if the person next to you has a head cold and wind it's going to really take a shine off things.

Sometimes you'll see "Special Buy" or "Special Purchase", "Special Price" items, they are all so very special. Often they are bulk bought items from the regular supplier with the brief of "the same stuff we normally get from you, only cheaper and not as good so we don't have people waiting to buy them every year instead of the full price stuff. Oh and we'll have thousands of them as well if that helps price wise." With these things it's all about expectations. Are you going to get those £70 Siberian Goose down pillows they have in stock all year round for £30? No, but you will get some really nice ones that you will quickly demote to the spare bedroom and visitors. When you say "Did you sleep alright?"

they will then reply "Yes! Those pillows were so comfy! Where did you get them?" and you can feel smug when you say "John Lewis" and they'll say, "Oh, you can tell, it's worth paying extra isn't it?" and you can say "for some things, definitely" like you're the most discerning purchaser of household goods this side of Which? magazine and they'll be thinking "They weren't that comfy" and "I only said they were good as a way to find out where she'd bought them and now I don't believe her anyway. She's not buying John Lewis pillows for the spare bedroom, not on her wage, I've seen the bread she buys."

There are things like say, glass and crockery where, in the real-use world, the difference in quality is negligible between the full and the special. Although I would say that when you work with these products all the time you can't help seeing the design of the special products as a sort of "homage" to the full price ones. A little bit like when you see those click-baity pictures of celebs in post cosmetic surgery and you think "Hmm. That looks just like X but why is her nose so thin?"

For me sale time is just a complete write off. It's that time when everyone concerned is kind of ok with everything looking a bit shit. I hate it.

I used to have a deeply felt dislike of anything that was "Sale", "Discontinued" or "Reduced". I would think "The market has spoken, this item is not good and worthless" or something like that. Now I realise that there are a myriad reasons why some things don't sell and get put into the sale. That buyer hit an extra zero on the order and now we're flooded out with more than people want, the boat with those deck chairs got held up and didn't arrive until the first frost, those water bottles that everyone was wanting while that reality tv show was on that everybody immediately lost interest in when it finished. But there are other times where it's a great product and, for whatever reason, the timing just isn't right. I've seen so many great product designs come in and just sit on the shelves before being reduced and forgotten. I really feel for the designers of these of these, and the buyers. Sometimes there just aren't enough customers with good taste around to make things a success (plus, I don't mind spending £12 on an oak and galvanised metal herb planter but £39? No mate, you are out of order. I am part of the problem, or rather my wage is).

CHAPTER 5

THE CUSTOMER IS ALWAYS

This chapter was originally going to be just a little collection of some of the amusing things that customers say and do in retail situations. A bit of soft chortle material with a wry eye roll, the kind of thing that might pop up on This Morning or The One Show. There will still be some of that at the end as a bit of a palette cleanser but in doing some research on this and asking some of my colleagues for their experiences on the shop floor the difference between how people interact with me and them was so stark that I had to reassess the content.

With the male contingent of our workforce the stories tended to be about things like argumentative customers, trying to fit 60 inch TV's into the back of Fiat 500's, shoppers still browsing when we're a minute from closing, that kind of thing. When I casually spoke to three female colleagues expecting roughly more of the same I was more than a little shocked when the first three experiences were -

"I was serving a couple who were buying a tablet and when the guy thought he was getting a good deal on it he held my face in his hands and squeezed my cheeks while his wife watched. She didn't react at all, I'm assuming he does it all the time."

"I was going through the specs on some tech for a couple and their son, I'd say he was about 12/13 and while I was talking he came up to me and started to undo my wrap dress. I had to take his hands off and redo the tie. His parents didn't say or do anything so I just had to carry on."

"I was talking to this guy about a laptop and I've got a tattoo down my back and I was wearing a white shirt and while we are talking he ran his fingers all the way down my back over my tattoo that he could probably just about see through my shirt as if it was the most obvious thing to do in that situation."

That was three people from one department with the first three stories they had. They were all more surprised at my shock than each others tales. I'm sure I'm shouting this into the void because I'm hoping that you aren't the sort of person that does this but, just in case, I think it's worth saying that just in general, not just in a shopping scenario, it is not ok to touch people you don't know. Just because they are being pleasant in telling you that you can upgrade the memory in your Lenovo laptop at a later date does not mean that this is an invitation for you to suddenly touch them like you are lovers you fucking psychopath. Perhaps there is some widespread niche of "shop porn" viewing that I'm unaware of that has some people bleeding their late night viewing habits into daytime reality.

In any case -

CUSTOMER TIP

DO NOT TOUCH THE PEOPLE WHO WORK IN THE SHOP.

Oh and while I'm here,

DON'T BE FUCKING RACIST TO PEOPLE WHO WORK IN SHOPS.

I'm a six foot one inch, white, heterosexual male. Apart from a fear of heights and occasional bouts of crippling depression and social anxiety I don't really have anything that impacts my ability to get through life without interference from others. I sit very much in the anonymous seat of facial attractiveness. My visage is not selling magazines but it's not appearing in Barnum's Victorian Travelling Freak Show either, it's just blandly hanging around on the front of my head. I've never thought of myself as being particularly lucky to have been dealt these haphazard genetics until recently. I grew up in a very rural white village, went to school without any cultural mix, went to a (from memory) largely white populated college, my first job was all white people, you get the idea. The one thing I thought I was blessed with was some innate sense of being working class and with it the idea that everyone should be treated fairly (bit of a leap there I know but I didn't exactly have a manual for my left leaning education). The teaching that things were shit enough for those without wealth without people making life hard for anyone else. This was further reinforced by a lot of the music artists I liked producing songs and doing concerts for equality, equal rights, anti-apartheid, workers rights etc. In my little bubble I assumed that now, post all this, that racism had now been confined to small groups of oddballs, social pariahs and fox hunters. Of course this was total shit. These moronic fuckers are everywhere, the only difference now is that they seem a lot more comfortable being twats in public.

The following is from a female colleague who, for this I will point out is not white, I worked with for several years and to my great shame, I had no idea that she suffered from this kind of brazen treatment from customers -

"I had a woman who came into the shop and was looking at laptops but then wandered over to the small electrical department get some help. They then directed her over in my direction. She came back over to my department to another colleague who was already serving a customer and they again pointed her over to me. I heard her say "What would one of them know? All the ones I've met are pretty stupid so I don't want to be served by one of them" I promptly left the shop floor, I don't get paid nearly enough to deal with that bullshit."

How about -

"I was serving a lady and she grabbed a fistful of my hair and pulled it pretty hard. When I confronted her she said, nonchalantly "Just checking to see if it was real. Your people don't tend to have real hair" and walked off."

I've described my friend here as "not white" which is a really horrible clumsy turn of phrase but it's because I've heard incredibly similar stories to this from everyone I worked with who isn't "white-european" looking. I'll say this for the bigoted racist customers we get, they aren't picky, they're a broad church when it comes to irrational hatred. Let's not forget, these people aren't just customers, they're employers, managers, father's and mother's who are happy to talk about "your people" and not being served by "one of them" so they'll be equally at home shaping the views of their kids and only employing people they feel happy being around. I didn't think I'd still be considering this as an issue when I was a teenager in the 80's but here we are. Racism is nothing if not resilient, in the apocalypse there'll be nothing left but cockroaches and bigots.

I obviously have no answers or advice on how to change any of this so what I would like you to take away from this is the sense that I am a really great guy for worrying about it occasionally.

Nobody who works with customers enjoys people taking the piss with returns or complaints but they do provide a bit of flavour to the day. Working in a shop that does try it's best to appease most requests does lead to the odd situation like when a customer returned blender that she said was faulty, complete with half blended soup in it. When we said it didn't look like a model or brand we sold she told us that it had been a gift from her friend so she didn't have the receipt but she had been assured that they had definitely purchased it from us and that she didn't want to stand around while we found out the details so she walked off to the cafe asking us to be ready with her refund when she returned. I get the feeling that if she'd had her fan or white gloves to hand there would have been an amount of wafting going on.   After some research we found out that the item in question was one of those limited offers from the centre aisle of Aldi. When she returned, satiated by a muffin and latte combo the assistant took absolutely no pleasure in informing her about the blenders origin before trying to hand it back to her. "Put it in the bin!" were her last words as she exited the shop, closely followed by her dignity, doing a little jog/walk. She couldn't even bring herself to enter an Aldi. I thought all the middle class had got over that phobia by now, "Of course I can't give up Waitrose for the main shop but Aldi do do some delightful Lebkuchen that were recommended in the Telegraph."

If you're going to go into a shop with "I know my rights" in your mouth just bursting to get out it's probably worth knowing your rights beforehand. I would say that the chances are that unless you're a moderator on the forums for MoneySavingExpert you're probably guessing at what your consumer rights are. Maybe you are still going by that time in 1985 that Joan complained about half of the packet of her Jacob's Cream Crackers being smashed into bird seed by the time she'd opened them at home and how when she complained they gave her a full trade size box, a bottle of Moet and a hand job as recompense for her distress. A lot of people understandably mistake a shops good will for their "rights". Most shops have their own guidelines for keeping customers happy that go above and beyond your consumer rights. At the end of the day they want you to leave happy and for them to have lost little to no money in the hopes you will return and spend, having told all your friends how you beat the system or gave the manager a piece of your mind after turning the checkout into your own "A Few Good Men" scene with you righteously, thunderously raging as the Tom Cruise character, leading the hapless military dinosaur Jack Nicholson assistant into your verbal trap.   In my long experience on the other side of the counter I would say it's always better to have a nice, reasonable conversation/negotiation with whoever is at the till to try and get what you want out of them.   Escalating your situation to the "I want to speak to the manager" stage is a lottery.   You probably won't get the manager, you'll get whoever is covering that floor that day (they will lie and say they are the manager or fluff it "I'm the manager in charge, yes") and on one hand you might get someone who will immediately give you everything you want and a £50 gift voucher on top for your trouble just because they are hungover and don't want to have to deal with your shit but equally you can end up with someone who treats any refund as a personal attack on their own bank account. Some people I've worked with delighted in the confrontational element and bestrode the floor to you with the attitude of a UFC fighter walking to the ring for their first title challenge, so it's really a better idea sorting out your problem with whoever is in front of you at the start. The other thing I would like to say (and I absolutely cannot stress this enough) is KEEP YOUR RECEIPT, KEEP YOUR RECEIPT, KEEP YOUR RECEIPT. Even if you just take a picture of it, it gives the shop so many needed details of your purchase and how they can best help you that it will save you 90% of the pain you'll have without it. It will say what you bought, where you bought it, how much you paid, who served you and what time you bought it.

The reason all of this is necessary is because shops have to deal with a very different type of customer. These customers don't like to pay for anything. They are not in the business of transactions, they aren't there to trade currency for goods and services. They are on the fucking rob, mate.

Shop lifters come in all shapes, sizes, classes and ages. I'm far from qualified to go into the socio economic reasons behind why people need to shoplift but I'm guessing I have chased more of them down the street than the writers of a thesis so I'll give you it from my point of view. The people who are robbing to pay for an addiction tend to go to where they would shop anyway which isn't your middle to high end shop because they've been prioritising the spending of their money on their stimulant of choice for a while and often personal hygiene and clean clothes have taken a back seat, this along with spatial awareness and the ability to look natural, being hampered by the effects of narcotics tends to make them stand out as potential shoplifter material in say Selfridges. This makes the lifters job harder so they'll aim for a softer target, the downside being that they'll have to rob three times as much because the value of the goods is so low.

There are "thrill seeking" shop lifters who presumably enjoy the adrenaline rush of the caper and the rush of getting away with that Boots Number 7 lipstick, just like in "Oceans 11". These often seem to think that if they weren't doing this they could probably do a job for MI6, when in reality that same adrenaline rush makes them twitchy and act like meerkats, always on the look out for security or staff which makes them stand out as obviously as the first category who has arrived at the shop on a mountain bike with dirty joggers tucked into black socks and a foil lined bag for life from Home Bargains.

The ones you are least likely to see are the professionally light fingered. They tend to work in gangs, often steal to order and are usually away on the motorway before you find those empty prongs where the Beats headphones used to be. These people would be absolutely great people to hire for a role in store security but they earn more stealing than retail pays so they don't fill in many applications.

I've worked with some really great store security/loss prevention/business protection (same thing in different guises). The kind of people you want to have your back if things turn tricky and have the staff and businesses best interests at heart. I've also worked with whole teams of security whose sole aim was to get as much stock from the shop floor into a transit van and on to eBay. Sometimes they were bright enough to procure the goods only to get caught having furnished there own houses with the ill gotten wares. For some reason this rankles me more than the other groups, especially when you've just done a ten hour shift dealing with customers and trying to stop shoplifters only to get bag searched on your way out by a Loss Prevention bloke who's also a super seller on eBay called *"xxBrandNewWithTagsxx"* with all the merchandise he's taking out of the loading bay on a night before locking up.

Businesses will often stress to the employees how much theft costs the company. How it affects the profit margin and how this is why the Bank Holidays will be paid at a flat rate. How you'll now have to start buying the uniform they expect you to wear and why they can't afford cleaners any more so you'll have to do that as well and how it's all basically your fault because you are letting the thieves get away with it (of course it is definitely not theirs for cutting security and shop staff who deal with these problems). Having shitter working conditions because people keep robbing you is annoying but then so is the mark up on a cup of coffee. If the thieves had more business acumen they'd set up an "artisanal" hot drinks stall outside and undercut the shop by a quid, they'd be minted in no time, might have to take on staff to deal with the rush, they might then start wondering why they're going through so many choc chip cookies now the new starter is working shifts on his own and doesn't seem to mind locking up at the end of the day.

I won't go into cafes, restaurants etc that are inside shops too much but I think it is worth saying that working in these environments must be similar to the kind of working experience that a trainee proctologist must face. As a customer you aren't in the best frame of mind, why would you be, you're dining in a shop? This leads you to not start off on the right foot with your food criticism. The coffee's not the kind you like, the scone is dry, there's not enough mayo on the sandwich, why are there so many seeds in the bread? I thought the panini might at least come with a salad for £7...and on and on. You are probably right in all these things. Most catering is built on providing the least they think they can get away with for the most profit, some do it better than others, some deficiencies can be overlooked if their muffins make your mouth smile from the inside or that tuna baguette is such a good combination of cucumber, mayo, seasoning, crisp outer bread and soft inner that it makes you forget the price. What I will say is that neither the price, the quality of the food or to some extent the service, is in the control of the people who've just served you and taken your money. That money is not going to them, it's going straight onto a spreadsheet for the head of catering to obsess over. All the people who I've worked with in catering for any length of time would never buy in the products that they serve, they all know better suppliers, better ingredients, the right levels of staffing to make it a pleasurable experience but they aren't the head of catering and they never will be because the food business is not about food at all, it's about the profit margin.

Having said that I have only worked in basic level retail catering rather than the kinds of places AA Gill would have waxed lyrical about. At the same time I've never shot a monkey so it's six of one etc.

What you will find, whether working in the cafe or the shop floor is that customer's do not want to know your name unless they are going to complain and give their tale of woe a bit of gritty realism by trying to out you as a shit. Even if they disguise it by saying "sorry, what was your name? Just so we can ask for you the next time we're in" means "What was your name? Just so we can firmly pin the blame on an individual rather than the faceless consumer mass when something, in our perception, goes wrong."

Men, I don't suppose you have ever been curious to know what it's like to have breasts (in this instance I am talking about what it's like to have them in a humdrum daily basis way, not on an "On your own in the shower" way) but if by some chance it has softly stroked your curiosity then wonder no more. Your thirst for learning can be quenched by simply wearing a name badge in a shop and talking to an increasingly frustrated and vexed customer who will not be able to consciously or subconsciously stop their little pupils from snatching furtive glances at your chest to see if they can piece together from those millisecond looks exactly what this prick in front of them's name is for the frankly furious email they will send as soon as they get home. I now realise how pathetic my teenage attempts at subterfuge were when I was trying to get enough glances at the hot girl who worked in the record shop's chest to mentally preserve for a few days. After several attempts by the customer of trying to furtively steal my chest information I would usually like to make things even more awkward by interjecting "my name is Rich by the way, in case you needed that for any reason". I didn't really need to do this, I have a face that could easily appear on a "Guess Who" game tile, so I couldn't really avoid being pinned by the customer in any angry email.

After several years of this I just stopped wearing a badge. It's a shop after all, not speed dating. If you need my name you can ask, you know, just like in real life. I decided I would start wearing a name badge if every customer did or if they paid me a professional footballers wage when I would happily have my moniker emblazoned across the back of my shirt. I had the same approach to wearing a uniform i.e. I didn't. I would wear something that looked close to the uniform but not quite. Uniforms in shops are always a bit shit. There are too many different shapes, ages and sizes of people to design a range of clothes that everyone looks good in and feels comfortable. Most stores get around this by making uniforms so dreadful that absolutely no one looks good in them so at least they have the consistency they were seeking in the end. I got round the uniform problem by behaving like a child. I would wear my own clothes, get a ticking off and told to wear the uniform, both my productivity and standard of work would plummet, I would then reintroduce my own clothes and my work rate and quality would go back to high before we we repeat the whole process again until the correlation between me being a better more valuable employee when I was wearing my own clothes was firmly set in their minds and an unspoken agreement was reached.

I think I was both a joy and a fucking pain in the arse to manage, hopefully not in equal measure. This may or may not explain why my work colleagues over the years have always seemed more than happy to tell me what their assessment of me and my character is. These aren't in a "I think this might help your development going forward" way. These are very much "I've formed an opinion about you and I very much feel the need to let you know what it is" way.

For example -

"I always thought you were a bit of a dick, but you're not."

"I used to think "God, he always looks such a miserable git" but when I talk to you, you aren't really. Well, nowhere near as much as you look anyway."

"I've worked with you for ten years and always thought you were a humourless miserable sod, but you can be quite funny sometimes."

"I didn't used to like you" - this one was often left without any resolution so you can make up your own minds as to whether the rest of the sentence was "...and I still can't bring myself to change my mind" or "...and now I just don't feel anything."

Not content with telling me these things and more, I would get the same comments several times from the same people. I get it. You used to think I was a dick. I don't really know what I'm supposed to do with the generous gifts you've given me but you can stop now and maybe spread your love around somewhere else. If I'd have known these opinions at the right time I could have brought them up in my end of year conversations with my manager "Lot's of people I work with used to actively dislike me, I was almost a hate figure, there was talk of a lynching at one point but now...well, not so much. Can I have a raise?".

CHAPTER 6

EAT THIS

It doesn't matter how big or small the size of the shop or department store you work in is, one of the things that can make or break inter personal relationships is when and how long people take for their breaks. Some of the fractures in colleague relationships could not be fixed by Mo Mowlam (for those of you under 40 you could use Davina McCall or Stacey Dooley instead) all because that bitch Sarah thinks that because she had to go for her break 15 minutes later than she was down on the rota for, then that means she gets 15 minutes longer on her break! No Sarah you fucking imbecile, it means you get the same length break, it's just later in the day! Every fucking time she does this! I can't make out whether she's just crafty or thick. Judging by that vacant look on her boyfriends face when he drops her off in the morning I'm going to go with thick, they tend to stick together don't they?

Because retailers always work out the amount of staff needed to effectively run a shop on the basis that nobody has a break because it makes the figures look better, this means that when you want to go for a break you have to wait for whoever else is having their lunch to come back first or there will be nobody on the shop floor serving. So, when you are hungry/bored/ knackered and Shaun decides that his half an hour break shouldn't have to include the time it takes to walk off or back onto the shop floor, any time getting his stuff out of his locker or any toilet time, you are now not eating at 1pm, it's going to be more like 1.20 or 1.25. Now you're hangry and pissed off at Shaun, so your half an hour now turns into 45 minutes as well. Now Kirsten who is going after you is going to be half an hour late for her lunch but you reconcile this in your head by thinking "well, she didn't start until 10 anyway so she shouldn't need to eat that early". Yeah, fuck Kirsten who hasn't stopped since 7 that morning, sorting the kids out and getting the food shopping in before work. Fucking Kirsten and her need for food, maybe she shouldn't have had kids and then she wouldn't be hungry at a normal hour. Stupid bitch.

All these irrationalities happen whether there are 2, 200 or 2,000 of you working in a shop because you no matter the overall size you're all broken down into smaller teams and these smaller teams create bigger frictions. I once worked in a shop where there was only two of us and someone from another branch used to come over and cover dinners which basically involved him nodding his head whilst we took it in turns to tell him in detail what a dick the other one was while they were on their lunch break. My list of complaints about him would often include -

I didn't like his glasses or the way he cleaned them or the face he pulled whilst he cleaned them.

His hair. That's not product on there. You just haven't washed it for three weeks.

The bobbles on his jumper. We work in a clothes shop mate, sort your shit out.

The way he read the paper first thing in a morning. He would breathe loudly on certain news stories.

The way he would stand with his arms folded at the front door when it was quiet as if he was determined to extend our run of no customers for the last hour.

His shoes which looked like the Clarks Commandos shoes that schoolboys would wear in the 1970's. He was in his fifties for fucks sake.

The way he would tut and shake his head at something but never say what.

He probably didn't have any gripes about me because I'm just an all round easy going great guy. At least he never mentioned anything to me. The point being that usually annoyances about your co-workers can be avoided or ignored during the majority of the day but come break time all bets are off.

It's the same story with booking your time off, you can guarantee that the one time you need a specific week off someone will decide that it's a matter of life or death if they don't have that particular week off instead of you. Once they get back from their mission from God and you ask them if they enjoyed the time off they will without fail say "Yeah, it was alright. Didn't do much." At this point it would be tempting unleash a verbal tirade on the selfish dick but there is the equilibrium and dynamic of the team to think about so it's far better to take a breath, walk away, let the anger pass and then over the course of the next three months make a note of every time they are late for work before passing it on to their line manager under the guise of being "concerned that they might have some problems at home."

It's impossible to get on with everyone. I learnt this when someone who I genuinely think is one of the nicest people in the country never mind my shop was described as "sly" by a friend.

"What do you mean, *sly*?"

"There's just something about her, I don't know, like she's hiding something? Nobody is that nice. Plus I don't like her voice.   Sing-song, Annoying."

And from then on the nicest person in England's character began to slowly, irrevocably decay in my mind.   Nobody *is* that nice.   I wonder what she is hiding?   Actually, now I think about it her voice it does quite get on my tits.   Who the fuck does she think she is?   Stuck up Disney voiced prick.

Some department stores have formal/informal social clubs to generate team spirit. Their activities can include things such as pub crawls with a fun theme that encourages people who don't drink regularly to "let their hair down" and "relax outside work" and "experience what it's like for everyone to have my drinking problem for a night". They also might organise trips to Blackpool where you can experience that same drinking problem in a place with a chronic drugs and poverty issue. You can also experience the highs of the rollercoasters and the uninvited lows of seeing a strangers genitals in the street before retiring to a hotel room you'd never normally accept as reasonable accommodation before getting on a bus the next morning to talk about the experience in the same way you might talk about a particularly distressing documentary about the proliferance of cock fighting in Mexican drug cartels. Also, two members of the bus party don't know it yet but they are both now parents. I don't get involved in any of these events for a variety of reasons. I'm a cultural snob, less so than I used to be but still, deep down I'm BBC4 not ITV2. Even though I don't watch either. My tolerance for organised fun begins and ends with sport. I like the fact that other organised fun exists (I'm not a complete sociopath), I like seeing audiences on TV shows seemingly get so involved in the light entertainment that they react as if Paddy McGuinness has just slotted home the winner in the Champions League final when he says "No Likey?"however I also likey being able to turn it off and not be there.

Sometimes there'll be a feeling that quieter members of the team need a little encouraging to let their hair down with a drinking game. I've never been one to need an excuse to drink. If I want a drink in a social setting I'll have one, I don't feel the need to have to roll a six or remember to put a nonsense word after every noun in a sentence. One of the reasons I've never understood drinking games is that the jeopardy consists solely of having to have a drink if you lose, but I *want* to have a drink, even if it's just to get me through this bit of the night. So if it's only a success for me if I'm shit at it, what's the point? Obviously the point is that drinking games were devised to get people who feel some shame in drinking to excess by their own volition. "It wasn't my choice to yam down twenty units of alcohol in half an hour before giving my manager a lap dance that would normally command a credit card sized appearance fee. It was Fizz Buzz" or whatever other horrific audience participation game. I am a bit competitive, less so now that I'm older, not because I am wiser, more because I'm a bit shitter at everything, so if the drinking games jeopardy was not having a drink if you fail then you would have found me heavily invested. I would probably turn up in a sponsored shirt with my name and number on my back.

I used to have a large dose of social anxiety so a large dose of alcoholic consumption was the self medication to get me to the requisite levels of relaxed and confident. I didn't usually achieve this successfully, of course I didn't, I was my own doctor and therapist and I was both entirely unqualified and patently drunk on the job. Say what you like about drug dealers but if you get a good one they'll know what to take and how much to get you to the right level of fucked up, you won't get that kind of insight from Geoff in Bargain Booze.

An element of organised fun that has always puzzled me is that part of the night when there is a dance floor involved and a song comes on and everyone gets up and does a synchronised pre choreographed dance, let's say for example the "Macarena". Where does everyone learn this? Do they see it on TV and practice at home? Do they go to so many of these events that they learn it from experience? It's a bit more obvious when the song is basically a line dance in disguise "slide to the left, slide to right, criss cross!" But otherwise I find it a mystery that I should never know the answer to.   It probably involves a drinking game and audience participation and for that reason, I'm out.

The other side to all this are the events away from both work and drinking - ten pin bowling, adventure Segwaying, paint balling etc.   These are usually held during the week and in locations far enough removed from civilisation that everyone is driving.   A sober event with work colleagues always has that taste of corporate team building and I can never quite shake the feeling that at some point I'm going to have to get everyone in the area gathered round so I can tell them three things about me and then try and build a raft from polystyrene blocks and swimming noodles with four people I don't like.

In case it isn't entirely apparent, I am a lot of fun.

Within the work place there would often be some scheme dreamt up by someone incredibly well meaning who worked in head office at a time when they were flush with cash and didn't mind giving someone 60k a year to find ways of "empowering staff". These people largely don't exist in the retail sector where it's rightly considered a waste of everyones time empowering staff only to lay them off in six weeks. They now write thought pieces for mindfulness app developers and books about empowering staff that they can then sell to the same businesses who don't mind spending £6 instead of six thousand for the same ideas. In several places I worked there would be a scheme in place to allow staff to be rewarded on a one off basis for good work over and above what was expected of them during the previous month. In some shops it would be for the staff themselves to vote for the recipient and in others the managers would get together and decide.   In either scenario the only thing that everyone could agree on each month was that the wrong person received the award.   It didn't really matter who got it and for what reason, there would always be sizeable part of the team that would clap at the announcement before slagging that decision off.

Clap, clap, clap, clap,

"Are they fucking kidding? The only reason she got all those accounts is because she never gets her fat arse off the till"

Clap, clap, clap, clap,

"If they're going to give it to her they might as well give one to that cleaner who hasn't been in since she slipped on that yogurt pot lid in the canteen"

Clap, clap, clap, clap,

"It's a joke. Everyone knows she's only got it because she's so far up Tom's arse he's got two tongues"

Clap, clap, clap, clap

"Well done Anna, thoroughly deserved!"

In one sense it did bring everyone together. It brought them all together to think "Why the fuck didn't I get that?". One nation under a mood.

There is a certain amount of recency bias involved but I can only recall one instance where someone received an award that was universally popular.   The recipient was incredibly hard working, diligent, helpful to all her colleagues, universally popular and always tried her best to get things right.   When the claps came they were genuine and with no adverse comments in-between. It was honestly thoroughly deserved.

Although I can't help feeling that, as I write this, I probably should have received that award as well. Not instead of obviously, but still.   I mean don't get me wrong she was really good and everything but *that* much better than me?   I don't know, I think it at least it needs re-looking at. I'll just drop them an email while it's fresh in my mind.

CHAPTER 7

TAKING STOCK

What could be less fun than have complete strangers enter a building you work in unannounced to verbally berate you for being part of a conspiracy to make, specifically their, lives intolerable by not including the charger in an electrical appliance that specifically states that the charger is not included and that was told to them when they bought it because surprisingly you aren't the first person to mention it so we now tell everyone to avoid this very situation? I'll tell you what's worse, how about counting every single item in the shop? That's right my dear customer. Just imagine that the next time you go shopping. At some point the people in there will have had to spend interminable hours counting the folded jumpers, cotton reels, rolls of wallpaper, books and nail varnish remover you've just wandered by. All while the shop is closed so it's either at night, early in the morning or both.

Sometimes if I'd been working ten hour or twelve hour overnight shifts counting the vast miscellany, I would get back home and go to bed with half a bottle of Cabernet Sauvignon and watch breakfast TV. It was the nearest I came to feeling like David Bowies character in The Man Who Fell To Earth. Then I'd have an unsatisfying daytime sleep with dreams about numbers and counting before getting up to go to work to do numbers and counting. Sometimes you'd have to work in pairs. You really have to get on with the person you're doing that with because by three in the morning you will want to smother them with one of the 252 pillows you've been counting before doing the same to yourself an hour later.

I'm a headphones person when I'm on my own. I'm always listening to things on headphones, music, podcasts, audiobooks, sports commentary. If I'm alone and not listening to things on headphones I'm either asleep or watching TV and even then when I'm watching TV I'm probably thinking it would sound better through headphones. This is largely due to my less than perfect hearing and the fact that I like my brain to be distracted from my unhindered thoughts at all times, no good can come from my free running brain neurones. I only mention this because if I'm spending hours counting stock then I will alternate through the different listening media. Maybe start with commentary from an evening kick off European match before a specially curated stock taking Spotify playlist and then into several podcasts I've saved up especially for the occasion. The task though is so tedious that even with my personally selected entertainment by 4 a.m. I am mentally telling the podcast hosts to fuck off, that audiobook narrator that their delivery is wooden and Laura Marling that, well in fairness she can just carry on, I'm just not in the mood right now.

I once worked for a chain of large department stores that decided that it was a waste of time and money to have us all counting socks at midnight when we could be selling them during the day. They also didn't trust the accuracy of our counting (we all felt very empowered by this judgement). So they hired a company that just went around and did stocktakes. "Great" we all thought "no more wine with breakfast news." The only fly in this particular Creme de la Mer ointment was that Head Office didn't trust the stocktaking firms counting either. This paranoia was possibly driven by a combination of cheap, easily available coke and the kind of Stasi blame culture that often crops up in competitive Head Office environments. I'm guessing; it's not for me to say, but it was. What our retail overlords decided was the best solution to this conundrum was for us to come in on a night and check the work done by the stocktaking firm. So here I am again, still listening to headphones in the middle of the night, still drinking a dry white at 6.30 a.m. (it compliments the Warburton's small toast, cutting through the rich butter) while watching ITV breakfast (it's less demanding in that situation than BBC) only now I get to watch a chap called Pavel count packs of mens briefs just before I go and do exactly the same thing to check he's got it right. I'm not a numbers person. I find them joyless, the numbers not numbers people. It's why I'm half decent at a spreadsheet, a lovely tool to deal with all that functional stuff. But I am capable of counting items. Pavel is pretty adept at counting items too, so good in fact that people pay him specifically for his counting abilities. I can, at a push, understand that you might not trust me to do your counting. Here I am a numerical amateur, a Johnny-come-lately in the adding world, by no stretch of the imagination would I class myself as a "professional counter" who would? I'll tell you who would - Pavel. Pavel would because that's literally his job description. Given our relative merits and abilities, in this scenario of counting things, who would you chose to be the counter and who would you have to check that their work is correct? I know, I know, you're right of course, you wouldn't have two of us doing it in the first place when you've already decided that I'm not up to it to the point that you've paid for a professional counter. The thing is you aren't thinking like someone who has never worked in a shop before and you have to make a decision now that won't drop you in the shit when the loss results come back and... fuck me it's half two on Friday and you'll never get back home in time to get changed and get out to Gigi's at this rate. So when the choice is either A or B then the safest option is surely both. Cannot go wrong.

And that is how you end up with me and Pavel both counting multi packs of mens briefs at 4 in the morning. Him, a pro counter counting and me, an unseeded wildcard entrant checking to see if he's done it right. I'm only surprised they didn't hire another counter to check my checking. Pavel said it was an absolutely farcical situation and then ten minutes later I checked his statement and agreed. When all this counting is done then the results of all this adding are analysed and blame is proportioned with the reasons for such poor results being -

Theft from shop lifters and staff working in the shop.

The shop didn't complete the admin correctly when the stock was delivered.

Items got broken or damaged or returned and the admin was done incorrectly by the shop.

The shop staff can't count.

The shop staff can't check other peoples counting.

It's the shop! The shop! The fucking shop!

Some or all of these can and will be factors. I will though give you a couple of examples of other factors that might hinder the accounting process.

I recently worked for a multi million pound company whose system was set up so that if, for example, a large L-shaped six seater sofa of considerable value went through the buying system and the delivery system but, crucially, didn't actually physically arrive in the shop and no reason for it's absence could be found, then it was just automatically added to the shops inventory. Everybody believed it was there apart from us who knew it wasn't, In the main because it wasn't. Nobody could be arsed dealing with this until we put through our stocktake figures and then you'd get emails asking how you could lose a massive sofa.

"We didn't lose it, it was never here"

"It was, it's on my spreadsheet. I can send a copy to you."

"Unless it's going to turn into the physical manifestation of a sofa I wouldn't bother"

There are lots of reasons why the sofa didn't turn up. Maybe it never left the factory. Maybe nobody checked Pavel's counting at the distribution centre. Maybe nobody asked the delivery driver if he'd found that him and his five family members were now sitting a lot more comfortably recently. Maybe the IT system was buggy, antiquated and entirely unfit for purpose. All of these things required effort and difficult conversations so in the end it's a lot better for everyone if they just carry on thinking that the shops are full of innumerate thieves. Sometimes the items never existed at all, but did, but didn't. How about attempting to buy 40 light bulbs but key in 400, realise your mistake, correct it and now you know you've ordered 40, the supplier knows and sends the shop 40 but the system still thinks you sent the shop 400. That would be stupid wouldn't it? Especially because now you'd have someone asking you to go and find 360 light bulbs that never physically existed. That would stump even me and Pavel and Pavel's supervisor Julie, who I never saw smile once and I could easily empathise with.

CHAPTER 8

PLEASE PLACE YOUR CAREER IN THE BAGGING AREA

It used to be easy to imagine that the high street institutions were all slick operations and their biggest concerns were getting that seasons collections right. In reality most are cobbled together over the years from a transient mixture of the talented and the talentless. A few too many years of the talentless and you're

labelled a "troubled retailer" in need of "saving".
Everything you do thereafter is under scrutiny.
It's surprising just how much of an industry
there is around failure. Accountancy firms,
liquidators, auction houses, re-sellers, training
firms, employment agencies, payday loan
lenders, they all hugely benefit from a retailer
going down the pan and your subsequent job
loss. It also keeps a couple of journalists in copy
for a few weeks if not more with "Can Jane Doe
turn the ailing high street stalwart around?" and
how "Christmas 20XX is going to be make or
break for John Doe Shop so let's have a look at
what they'll be selling us" with the attitude to the
products often being dictated by whether John
Doe Shop's PR team have paid the particular
media enough money to say nice things or not
hence "£40! For this! No wonder they are going
under! They've lost touch!" in one paper and
"This is exquisite and the ideal gift, beautifully
packaged and an absolute steal at £40" in
another.

When you work in retail for an extended period of time it is inevitable that for one reason or another you won't be working for that employer any more. You'll get a better offer or opportunity and leave, your shop will close, the business will fold, you will realise the futility in the struggle for little reward and leave to take up dry stone walling, the reasons are myriad. That doesn't though compare with losing your job because the business is failing, whether you can see it on the cards or it comes as a shock. I've been unfortunate over a near thirty year career in retail to have it happen three times and it never gets any easier. That feeling of knowing that no matter how well performed, how hard you tried, how dedicated, that you're no longer wanted, no longer needed. Financially they would be a lot better off without you around. There's also a huge sense of uncertainty, now what's going to happen to me? Will I get another job? Can I survive until I get another job? If I do get another job what will it be like? Will I still see my friends from work?

It really is frightening and fucking horrible. I've been pretty scathing about Head Office and senior management previously and that is because of my previous experiences with shop closures and job losses. When you work in a shop and you are so reliant on others getting things right, the right product delivered at the right time with a price that doesn't make it impossible to sell. Having the budget to employ the right number of people to make it work. The right decisions being made on what to invest in and what direction the business will go in. All things you can't control on the shop floor but that can have such an impact on how well you can do your job. It speaks volumes about the current state of retail that the last swathes of job losses in retail have included Head Office staff which are usually almost the last to go. So when

I see the idiocy of the decisions made by the heads of these institutions I find it absolutely infuriating, not because they get things wrong, we all do (although some decisions beggar belief) but because they're made from a position of no jeopardy, no accountability. There is no "How will I survive without this job if this goes wrong?" for them. If you are working for a part-time minimum wage in retail (retails favourite kind of worker) you already aren't on a living wage, throw some debt into the mix and losing your job doesn't mean that you'll have to let the holiday cottage go and the youngest might have to go to that nice state school that had some very good Ofsted figures last year instead of the public one your eldest went to. It means you are fucked. Absolutely fucked. That is real accountability and jeopardy so if you are a "Senior Figure" and your sales staff give you a bit of shit for your decision making over the previous year then you should should just take it on the chin and listen.

Speaking of listening, which I think is an incredibly powerful tool (that's my blisteringly new look at taking on board other peoples views) I recently worked for a business that was very keen on the idea of listening. Listening to the sounds of their own voice, us listening to them, that kind of listening. We had lots of forums and online communities where we could listen. Isn't it great about how much listening is going on? It makes a good media soundbite as well. "We're a company that treats listening as a vitally important part of our business." I hate to pop your instagram filter here but listening is important to all businesses, even the chronically shit, evil ones. I'm pretty sure that a point near the top of every dictators list of things he wants people to do is "Listen very carefully to every fucking word I say, or it's a swing on the lamppost ride for you", it doesn't make them good leaders and it doesn't make them good employers. When the listening membrane only flows one way it gets very annoying very fast.

I'm actually kind of ok with businesses being dictatorial as long as they're open about, at least you know where you are with "look mate, just shut up and do it", there's a clarity of thought. What really twists my tits is the "We're more like a family than a business" line, which is true if you mean one of those families that social services have to consistently bring up in their weekly agenda.

Within these inclusive forums and online communities you would find that any negative or even less than positive comments would be removed or passively aggressively challenged to the point where discourse disappeared, meaning that ill advised schemes would just be snow plowed through in a drift of niceness until they ran off the edge of the cliff because nobody felt willing or able to mention that the road ahead had collapsed. As an example there was a merchandising online community that was set up by merchandisers in various shops, to share ideas and solutions to problems, you know, the kind of thing a regional manager gets paid to do but doesn't. Word of this subversive activity got out and so Head office decided to combat this by setting up their own OFFICIAL COMMUNITY which we all had to subscribe to and no longer use the unofficial one. The first difference to this community was that that we mere plebs who actually did the work on the shop floor were no longer allowed to post and share examples of good work, only the regionals and head office could now do this (these being the same people who hadn't done any of this previously) and any unauthorised posts or comments would be removed. So they took away our voice and replaced it with theirs and skipped lightly with their eyes closed over the definition of "community" whilst they did it. A little message to all of you happy, inclusive businesses who don't have an outlet for criticism and critique from your work force - If you're so afraid that your ideas won't stand up to their scrutiny, maybe they aren't great ideas in the first place?

Kicking against the door and taking it to *the man* might seem like the right heroic thing to do. Of course it's not, it's the stupid thing to do because -

None of your grievances will be listened to.

Nothing would change.

You are now marked out as a problem and a disruptive influence that needs to be dealt with.

If you harboured any notions of career progression you will now have to pop your little notions into your back pack and take them somewhere else.

In reality, disturbing the waters not only means that you won't be moving onwards and upwards it also means that where you are now will probably get more difficult. Fear not though, there might, however be a solution and it lies in how you frame your complaint.

"It's just so frustrating when we were all discussing a packaging issue and how we could save both money and resources for the business on the old open community!"

"I found a way of saving time on installation that would mean we could help out more on the tills at the busiest periods but I didn't know who to take it to now the comments section has been removed!"

That kind of shit. It puts them in an impossible position because they can't then be seen to disagree with something they've been advocating for. They might hate you for it but they will admire your cunning and use it for themselves elsewhere . As a side note you don't have to have any real facts or numbers to back up your claims, they really won't be bothered to check, it's amazing how easy bullshitting is when everyone is doing it.

My most recent employ was cut short when my shop was closed. This was due to a few reasons -

Not enough people with not enough money in the area.

Amazon

Brexit

Global Pandemic

Every other online retailer

Poor management

Amazon

When my shop became surplus to requirements, so did I. In the run up to my career demise we were visited on several occasions by the great and the good from senior management. This was to express their sorrow at the situation and to hear what we thought went wrong and what could be learned for the benefit of the remaining shops. This did all feel a little bit like discussing family planning options just as the baby's head starts to appear, but still, the thought was there I guess. We had so many VIP's visiting to say how sorry they were and how awful it was that it was like attending a two month long wake, with the buffets that were laid on each visit adding to the sad air. One of the phrases that came up often was how they were all so "Sorry to be visiting you in such sad circumstances" especially as it was the first time any of them had visited us.

"I'm sorry to hear troubles you've had" I would say in our meetings "It's not been on the news or anything. I know we would have made some kind of effort to find a way to help if we'd known that there aren't any current means of transportation between London and the North of England."

"I'm sorry?"

"Well we have been here for years and nobody previously bothered visited us to ask our opinion on anything and now we're closing you are queuing up to get in, so I'm assuming the old checkpoint is now open and you can move freely up and down the M40."

This would have been a brilliant slam, a witty retort to the Bosses in front of an admiring crowd of fellow shop workers. Sadly the karaoke microphone we were using didn't have much of a reach and kept breaking up so when she said "I'm sorry?" It wasn't because she'd fallen into my satire web, it was because she couldn't hear me and by the time I'd walked to the front to regain reception to the wireless microphone and repeat my barbs both the moment and my comedic timing had gone. Still, I think the point is valid.

Now that "High Street Retail" is rapidly becoming a niche industry, like Microlight manufacturing or fags, there are different expectations on the people who work in them. Where once you might find specialists with different areas of expertise or responsibility, now you will find that the shop will still want you to have that same expertise, just in everything, all at the same time and for the same money.

Department Manager: "You know how Dave does all that IT stuff?"

Sales Assistant: "Yeah, I don't know how he knows all that tech stuff."

Dept Mgr: "Well you will because I think you could do that, easily, so I've booked you on some training courses."

Sales: "Oh God, really? I'm not very technically minded..."

Dept Mgr: "Don't worry, it's all simple.   It's basically turning things off and on again. In fact I reckon you could do the till set ups and banking as well."

Sales: "What? But that's Janices job, she's the supervisor!"

Dept Mgr: "You're a quick learner, that's why I've got you in the Bracknell store for a week learning how to do her job. You're in that nice Premier Inn with breakfast on me so never say I don't treat you."

Sales: "Shit. What pay grade will I be on? They're both on higher ones because they're specialists."

Dept Mgr: "It'll be the same money for you but you will now be a "Global Specialist" with responsibilities right across the shop. All exciting stuff."

Sales: "What? So I do the same job as them and they get more money than me? That's not fair."

Dept Mgr: "You're damn right it's not fair. That's why we're making them both redundant. They do say Bracknell is beautiful in the Autumn, like Fall in New England. Don't forget to make the most of that breakfast."

Businesses can avoid this press ganging approach by encouraging people to be multi skilled when times are good. Lots of people would really like to learn new skills, whether to stretch their minds a bit, break up the humdrum bits of their normal job, or to find out just how much Dave is taking the piss when he says it will take him three days to fix that printer or when he runs "diagnostics" with solitaire. It's a lot easier to sell these options as just that, options, rather than leaving it until the desperate last minute with a "Do it, or we're all fucked"message. This kind of pre planning for tough times doesn't usually happen. Businesses get cocky and self congratulatory with a run of success. Are you telling me that the retail geniuses behind that wedding gift promotion and those new bikini and pool wear ranges could ever be in the shit? Do me a favour. What's that you say, no weddings or holidays for two years because of a global pandemic? Well at least we can cash in on garden furniture, only some really quite piss poor parking by a container ship in the Suez Canal could stop that.

In fairness these are extremes and I wouldn't expect anyone to have put money on these things happening, especially together. It would be like having a double bet on both Leicester winning the Premier League and Donald Trump becoming President of the USA. But Brexit wasn't exactly an overnight disaster and the rise of online shopping away from physical shops has been obvious to everyone for years and yet nobody seems to have cracked these two issues.

The general assumption from people outside the shop floor is that anyone can do retail work, it's not skilled, but then times get hard and you have to reduce your workforce and have fewer people to do more roles and all of a sudden you need really good people to keep this thing afloat, but you aren't paying any more money for the harder work and stress involved so there is no incentive for the good people to stay.

And you wonder why it's so hard to recruit people?

The company that I worked for had a lot of unfilled vacancies and struggled to maintain day to day staffing levels in some shops, even while it was laying off staff in other shops. The thing is the hours might not work for you for child care, transportation etc, your journey might be twice as long (nobody is paying you for that time lost, sat on that shit bus everyday) and you're working for people with a track record of laying people off, which doesn't help your stress levels or quality of life and planning for the future. For so long these businesses have been used to selling a retail dream to customers and have no idea how to sell a retail career to potential employees. Now they are going to have to use those same customer selling skills to get staff through the door, free lunches, extra days holiday, more flexibility with hours, bigger staff discounts. On the flip side of all this you can have the most amazing set of candidates, robust interview procedures and a round table discussion on your final decision and still end up employing an absolute bell-end.

Here are just some of the "characters" I have worked with -

Two people who, over the course of several weeks, "toileted" in a bucket outside, leaving it to desiccate in the summer heat before putting the now powdered contents into the air vent of a van that a trainee had to drive 250 miles in that day.

He blew up a TV at work and wasn't in a rock band.

He once rode in the goods lift all day, only stopping for his break and presumably travel/altitude sickness.

Sold vitamin pills as ecstasy tablets to colleagues. This obviously only worked once. Vitamins make you feel good but not *that* good.

Thought that the brown wire was Earth because it was brown. Like the earth. He worked on the lighting department and unsurprisingly once electrocuted himself whilst "testing" something with his finger.

On the phone to a customer he picked up a ruler to describe how big something was. He was on a landline phone.

Lost one of their five senses (they didn't).

Mentioned in their first week that they couldn't climb ladders and were allergic to cleaning products in a job that needed you to hang things from the ceiling and clean things on a daily basis. These weren't secret elements of the job.

Spraying a customer with room fragrance as if it was eau de toilette. She also carried a conker in her pocket as it "kept spiders away" so I think there were a few other issues to unravel there.

Unable to to talk to customers without crying. I did mine on the inside like any reasonable person would.

Whenever her head went back her eyes closed like on those old fashioned dolls. Not that much of an issue as long as she didn't need to get anything from high shelves. Whenever there is a solar eclipse I always think of her, safe in the knowledge that even if she was tempted she couldn't stare at it.

Being consistently late from lunch because they were addicted to gay saunas.

Smelling (general). So many smelly people.

Walked into the same glass panel next to the front door so often that we had to put trolleys in front of it to stop him breaking his nose, or worse, the window.

Regularly eating and drinking the food products in the stock room and then helpfully leaving the containers and wrappers on the shelf.

Calling people "flower" and "cock". I accept that these are acceptable dialect choices in some specific regions and are a term of friendly endearment ("Morning flower! How are you?" "Take care out there cock, it's icy on that pavement today!") but if you aren't acquainted with them they come across happily delivered insults.

Sitting in the middle of a fake foliage display in a restaurant in chefs whites and holding a large kitchen knife with the aim of jumping out at the next person who entered (he got bored and got out before anyone came in).

Being asked to leave because of your habit of turning up to work drunk and getting your revenge by leaving a Trip Advisor review saying the shop was infested with rats. On the plus side he never questioned the rats sobriety.

Needing to go home because of the anxiety they were suffering which had been brought on by their mum seeing ghosts. In fairness, who hasn't had a couple of days off for this?

A chap who worked in the warehouse who would shout everything he said. He was comfortably over 6 foot 6 inches, more in his safety boots, and appeared as a kind of roving human fog horn, warning off errant sailors who might end up dashing themselves on the rocks of the Kitchen Aid mixers if not for his sonic boom. I was convinced this was because of some faulty wiring in his brain or other unfortunate affliction and so didn't comment on it until one day I was sat with someone who'd known him for years and a new starter. The new starter had no such worries about offence and just asked "What's the deal with that bloke who shouts everything?" and it turns out there wasn't anything wrong, he just really likes shouting. Everything. All the time. That must have come up in his interview. Perhaps it was conducted on the deck of a busy aircraft carrier.

Locked themselves inside the cleaning cupboard to hide for a few hours.

Couldn't understand why when she received her first wage slip that we hadn't paid for her parking. We didn't pay anyones parking and besides that I'd seen her arrive on the bus.

Insisted on wearing safety gloves and a hi-vis vest when lifting anything heavier than a ream of printer paper.

There are many more examples, although I think a large proportion of these may have been the product of a terrible home life and/or mental illness and whilst I found them highly amusing at the time, for the sake of taste and decency I will refrain from recounting their foibles here. That said, if you catch me at the right time at the bar I will bang on about them for a good hour or so.

In an ideal world your career path would be dictated by your ability to do the role. It isn't of course, life isn't like that. The best team doesn't always win the football match no matter how well they play. Votes put to the general public don't always go the way that all fact and logic say they should (I really still cannot get over that). No matter how capable you might be and how well suited you are for the job you are going for there is always the human element that in the end will be the deciding factor. There are very few people making recruiting decisions that can remove that thought of "Do I want this person being around me everyday?" It is a valid question and part of your suitability for the role is how well you will fit in with your colleagues. If the job involves a lot of concentration, free of distraction and some of the words used to describe a candidate are "Bubbly" and "Vivacious" and they are "a lot of fun", then in the work place you might find the rest of the office describing them as "Loud" and "Annoying" and "if they don't shut the fuck up for five minutes I'm going to put them in a chokehold". I'm not making any judgements on the interviewers. I've been guilty of this myself when I've been in the same position. I've never thought "Are we going to be great mates?" or "Can I see myself going for a drink after work with this person?" I'm a pretty unsociable person so the answer in almost any situation is probably going to be no. No, what I am thinking is if this person can do the job well and can I tolerate them around me and the rest of the team every day? Tolerance is, as we have talked about previously, a much maligned attribute. In my own case, other peoples tolerance of my annoying character traits has enabled me to stay employed. They did this not because they particularly liked me, but because it was a reasonable trade off for the quality and quantity of work they knew they would get just by having to tolerate me around them for half an hour every day.

The Interviewer will also be thinking "Are they a [insert brand] type person?" Do you fit the brand image, do you represent what the shop is about? I know I've been passed over for a couple of jobs when I could do the job but didn't fit the image of the brand and that's fine. I've never bought any of their products and will bad mouth them at any opportunity but I'm broadly ok with their decision. It was probably for the best, although I have noticed a steady decline in their share price over the last four years so, maybe that's something for them to think about.

It is a fair element to consider. In my first managerial role I didn't have the luxury of being able to select a team of people who could have appeared in those adverts where all the staff have really great dentists. I had to go with the least worst options which resulted in a workforce who looked like The Wild Bunch (for younger readers lets say Suicide Squad, the David Ayer one not the James Gunn one).   I'm certainly not saying you should recruit people who only look a certain way.   Though if you're applying for a job that requires you to stand at the entrance to the shop wearing only board shorts and flip flops you're probably pretty confident you're going to get it. Apart from the very dark shops that sell American casual wear and smell heavily of their signature fragrance, most places don't need to just employ people based on their lucky genetics and dedication to a teenage workout routine. It's more about the attitude and how the staff carry themselves.   You can see it in the stores that sell very expensive items such as jewellery or watches (I'm not really sure why I felt the need to specify, I'm assuming you weren't thinking of elephants or oil rigs).   The staff in these shops have that kind of easy attitude that says "I don't need to sell you this stuff, look at it, it's all fucking amazing.   No, I'm here to help you choose *which* of the amazing stuff you are going to buy, because you obviously are, so we can all just chill out now that's out of the way". Funnily enough you can get that same attitude in pound shops, where you're definitely buying, it's just a matter of what and how much. It's the in-between shops where you get the attitude shift. These are the kind of shops that still have that "Sell me this pen" bit in their interviews. Let's take a high street retailer that sells, for example, electrical products for home use. When I visit I always feel like I've stumbled into a conference for charity street fundraisers. The TV's and washing machines are the by-products here because the margin on electrical items is minuscule, so it's all about the extras.

"Yeah, yeah, big TV, picture quality yaddah-yaddah. Can we talk about installation for a minute?" They'll say, uninvited "You'll want that wall mount, get it wall mounted, you'll definitely want a wall mount and get your soundbar set up, that's a separate extra but you'll want that. Have

I mentioned after care? You'll want that, what if it breaks? No, you won't be covered if it breaks accidentally, just if it spontaneously stops working with no outside factors, but that can happen, probably will, almost certainly will, it's just what these 6K TV's do, it's the price of being on the bleeding edge of technology. What about your old TV? Whose getting rid of that for you? We can recycle it, just a small extra charge but worth it to know that we've taken it away and sent it to a country that overlooks biohazards at the minute.   I've filled in a form for you for extended warranty. No, it's not the same as after care, it's different, it just is. Now let's just tot all that up and...wow, that's quite a lot. Luckily we do have flexible credit available, ordinarily it should take quite a bit of time to assess whether you are suitable for these credit terms but for reasons I won't go into I can get you approved in less than 2 minutes."

"I'm actually here for just a normal home printer?"

"Ah, then you'll definitely need a monthly ink subscription plan!"

I've seen this from all sides as I had an unfortunate six month stint working for a now defunct high street electrical retailer in their call centre. My very first call after training was from a customer whose laptop had stopped working and she could no longer retrieve any data from it and, as a journalist, needed it for work. I went through all the correct procedures which basically amounted to me saying tough shit, you are fucked in as nice a way as I could and at the end of the call she said "I know it's not your fault but the calmer you are and the nicer you are THE MORE IT FUCKING ANNOYS ME" and then hung up. In any reasonable retail scenario this would be an abject failure from start to finish but for this business, in this call centre, it was an absolute result. The call was relatively short, they didn't have to give her anything, it didn't cost them anything and they hung up. For a non-sales call this was perfect for them. Later that morning I had someone call me to say their washing machine was literally on fire and I had to tell them that I wasn't perhaps the first call that she needed to make and maybe deal with the fire incident first. That's all it was for eight hours a day, seven days a week. A constant stream of unhappy people, angry and desperate to get their problems sorted and my job was to solve or not solve it, it as long as it didn't cost anything and I didn't take too long (everything was timed, including our toilet breaks). I can't remember how many hours I spent in negotiations with people on how much recompense I was going to give them for the frozen food that they had been forced to bin due to a faulty freezer (in fairness I did leave there under the impression that I was the only person in East Yorkshire that didn't have a lifetimes supply of salmon and lobster ready to thaw out at any minute). One of the more pleasant outcomes of a call would be that the customer would become so frustrated and enraged that they would swear and then you could inform them that you would be terminating the call. I know half your house has burned down because of a blaze caused by a washer-dryer we sold you but because you called me a cunt when I told you you aren't covered I'm going to cut you off, which I'm sure will help you calm down and rethink your attitude to me and the service you've received.

Six months in and after a couple of weeks being sick every morning before work because of the stress I handed in my notice. They seemed quite surprised, not because I was leaving (they were very used to high staff turnover) but because if you made it to six months you'd generally be dead enough inside to not give a shit about what anybody said on the phone. Equal worst job I've ever had. Up there with the time I spent in a food processing warehouse on night shifts spading wheel barrows full of pink and white meat slop into an industrial burger making machine. On my first shift proper (after passing the training which seemed to consist entirely of pie top identification) I met my colleagues. Six, I'm going to say "sturdy and robust", women in our uniforms of white boiler suits, hats and black safety boots, greeted me by telling me they were going to rape me. I couldn't hear any banjoes or swamp enabled speedboats but I'm guessing they were around. On the plus side they did not require me to look good in board shorts and flip flops.

CHAPTER 9

WET FLOOR SIGN

If you have worked in retail for a reasonable length of time (I have decided how long reasonable is in this case but I don't think it's necessary at this stage to tell you. I think it adds some much needed mystery to the book) you will see the kind of variety of mishaps and accidents that keep some YouTube channels going for years. What look like perfectly capable human beings manage to make ascending and descending an escalator look a particularly difficult exercise from the SAS's selection process. Suddenly there are hazards I had previously not been aware of such as how to approach it and at what angle? How do I judge the speed of the steps to get on? When do I put my other foot on? How white do I need to make my knuckles when I'm gripping the handrail? How do I stop myself from falling backwards? Oh christ, we're nearly at the top, how do I get off?   I used to think of escalators as being "effortless stairs", I do not think this any more.

Small kids and old people absolutely love twatting themselves on escalators. They cannot wait to forget how to stand up. The results of all this are pretty grim. Although piss easy to use, escalator steps are particularly unforgiving to inherently wobbly people. A blunt cheese grater is still not a mattress so the emergency stop button is hit, there is a large amount of wailing, paramedics and first aiders are called and customers have to make the tricky decision to either a) move on and give them space to deal with the incident and give the victim some decency by not stopping to stare or b) gather round staring and saying how awful it is and how the same thing happened to Margaret in House of Frasers that time. It's B, always B. You will also then have to deal with a stream of customers coming into the shop, seeing the escalator is now out of action, and being utterly dumbfounded as to what they're supposed to do instead. I can only assume that they realise that there are stairs available but they had really been looking forward to gliding up the floors in a papal fashion and now having to use the normal stairs has really fucked up their whole day.

There's always the lift. This though has its own issues. I'm not entirely sure what some people expect when the lift doors open but it doesn't correspond with any lift experience I have ever had (and believe me, I have lifted). In a normal passenger lift in a shop I'd expect it to accommodate anywhere between 4 and 8 people, big enough to comfortably fit in a buggy or wheelchair. For some people however the expectation seems to be for a rolling expanse of summer meadow, or perhaps the ballroom at the Summer Palace, or maybe a wall of blue static that you pass through to emerge on the other side into the small electrical department accompanied by sounds created by the BBC Radiophonic Workshop. Whatever the expectation, the fact that it is the size of an average bathroom, sans furniture and towels, seems to suggest that it is a trap to lure select customers into an airless retail sarcophagus. Quite what we would get out of all these suffocated customers I don't know. We'd have to get an extra Biffa waste wagon each week at the very least, which is a far bigger annoyance than you'd think, if you ever had to.

OK, you're probably thinking to yourself, some people just aren't used to dealing with escalators and lifts, and you'd be right, but I will say that we have the same issue with stairs. Not some special shop stairs, just stairs, stationary steps if you will. They aren't camouflaged in anyway. None of them are fake stairs that will give way allowing the psychopathic killer to catch up to you. Disappointingly they don't light up when you stand on them either. If you're physically capable of tackling them then everyone has to have a first encounter with stairs, tricky as a small child when the steps aren't scaled for you but once you grow a little then they become second nature. You might even run up and down them. When I was child and lived in the middle of nowhere, descending the stairs in a different way was a big source of entertainment, sliding down them on my bum (clothed after the first burns), putting my socked feet on the very outer edges of the steps so I could descend in silence like a secret agent (it was actually like a ninja but I realise this may be interpreted as cultural appropriation - it was the 1970's, it was a different time. Ninjas were held in aspirational esteem, alongside firemen, cowboys and motorcycle daredevils). One of my favourites was to stand at the top of the stairs with my back to the drop, hold onto the bannister, put my socked feet onto the gloss painted wooden skirting boards that run up both sides of the stairs and then slide down, my speed controlled by my "hand brakes". Even though through excessive use my feet began to wear away a one inch strip of wallpaper just above the skirting, it was a small price for my parents to pay for the otherwise free amusement it gave. When even my backwards speed slide lost it's lustre, I took to jumping the last few steps to the bottom, first two, then three, you get the picture. This ended when I was attempting a leap from just over halfway up the stairs. I had not taken into account the angled drop of the ceiling, perfect height for if you are walking down the stairs, not so much if you are jumping down them. And so it was that that I crashed face first into the ceiling and then arse first down the stairs, prematurely ending what was probably the early birth of parkour.

My only other stairs mishap was on the night of the first of September, 2001. The reason I can be so accurate is because it was the evening when England beat Germany 5-1 in Munich and, to my great shame, I had become particularly inebriated at my local hostelry with some holidaying Geordies who had presumably migrated to Hull for the warm weather. I woke up in bed naked and in need of the loo, which was downstairs. I missed the first step and slid all the way down the carpeted stairs to the bottom, landed on my feet and walked nonchalantly into the bathroom. The next thing I remember were a series of loud explosions and when I opened my eyes I found myself in the dark on the bathroom floor holding a towel like a comfort teddy whilst the street oiks were letting off celebratory fireworks. So Michael Owen got a career defining hat trick and I got buttock burning carpet friction.

What I would say in my defence is that none of these occurred whilst shopping so when I do see a fully grown capable adult tumble down the stairs in my shop my first thought does tend to be "Oh, you've got to be fucking joking" just before phoning the first aider. The "Wet Floor" hazard signs and cones that appear in shops at the merest appearance of drizzle aren't there to warn you that the floor tiles might be damp, you know that already, you've just walked through the rain to get in and life experience has told you that wet people = wet floor possibilities. What the Wet Floor signs are actually saying is "Don't even think about throwing yourself on the ground and making a claim that your livelihood has now been lost because of damp coat distress." They should just have a permanent sign embedded in the floor at the entrance that says "If it is, or has been, raining, assume the floor may be wet in places" but I suppose someone would fall over whilst reading it.

It will not come as a surprise to anyone that there is notable proportion of people walking amongst us who assume that there is someone directly to blame for any unpleasant occurrence or annoyance that befalls them. For them the flow chart from "bad thing happening" to "person who is to blame" is short, clear and obvious to all. There are no longer offshoots to areas of nuance or common sense, this is no branch, this is a line. Let me give you a scenario, you are in a home furnishings shop or department and you are wearing a black coat, nothing unusual in that unless you are perhaps a Chelsea pensioner. On your stroll through the wares you spot a large decorative throw in a colour you've been looking for that could be perfect for your sofa. It's a subtle combination of white, cream and pale grey and has the texture of some kind of fantasy alpaca, it is hairy but with a softness that is comparable to that dream you had once were you were a kitten and your mothers paws enclosed you in a feeling of calm. How do you know the throw is the right size, first thing to do is ignore the label (it's in centimetres "Why can't they label them with "small sofa" medium sofa" etc?" you think) so the only thing to do now is to open it out against yourself and use your own physical dimensions as the rule "With my arms above my head I am sofa sized." Perfect! Now to fold it back up and take it to the...oh no, oh dear god no! Your black coat now looks like it has been worn by Santa's barber! It's ruined and it has now really soured your feelings towards the throw (Aunt Jeans cat "Sesame" did give your pre teen knee a rather vicious right hook once now you come to think of it).

"Someone must pay for this!" you think, you probably don't think that, I wouldn't but for this exercise you do. What you probably feel is a far more murky sense that something unfortunate has happened and without the hug of a mother and a reassuring "there, there, it's all ok" your emotions want to get back to the even keel they were at before. This could be by just taking a breath and putting it down to experience, laughing it off with a funny Instagram story "I felt like a muppet opening up this throw and now I look like one as well!" Laughing crying face emoji, hands over face emoji, monkey with hands over eyes emoji, stars. Or by finding justice over the inanimate object. Whichever seems the most emotionally mature at the time.

Customer: "I've just held one of your throws and now my coat is ruined. I want it dry cleaning and if that doesn't work I want a new coat."

Sales Assistant: "Oh no, let's have a look. Ah, I think we can get this off here."

Customer: "I don't think you can! You'll never get all that off! Why on earth would you sell something that does that to black coats?"

Sales Assistant: "I can see it's frustrating but I'm sure we can fix it here for you. Those throws are lovely but they do shed some hair initially, it mentions on the label to give it a shake and a brush before first use because of the fibre loss."

Customer: "Well I didn't see that, it should be on a sign not a label. So are you going to get it dry cleaned or give me the money to do it?"

Sales Assistant: "Let me try the lint roller first, just to see what we're dealing with."

Customer: "A lint roller won't get that off, ridiculous!"

Sales Assistant: "We have a special commercial version in the back, it's very good. I won't be a moment."

We don't have a special version, it's just an off the shelf clothes roller but there are times when you just need to stand in the back corridor for a couple of minutes to give the illusion that something greater is happening before returning with a hair free black coat, an offer of free coffee vouchers and a chance to purchase the throw with a third off because of all your trouble, all of which is accepted. As the previously wronged customer you now walk away with a story about how you've changed the company policy on hairy throws *and* got free coffee for bringing it to their attention *and* got a massive discount.

"You've just got to stand your ground Jen" you will say sagely over a hot chocolate, no cream, in Caffe Nero after Yoga Thursday "they respect you more for it."

We don't, we're just pandering to you because we've been on our feet all day and cannot be arsed entering into the inevitable "I'm writing to Watchdog!" dialogue. I'm a big proponent of consumer rights so when they are bandied about to use in cases of obvious bullshittery I find it infuriating especially when your short little flow chart shows us that you are hairy because of the shop and lack of signage, not because wrapping yourself in a moulting Llama whilst dressed as the bass player from the Sisters of Mercy didn't occur to be a bad idea.

CUSTOMER TIP

If you have a genuine issue or concern try and make sure you voice it at the time rather than later when the moment has passed if you can. Give them a chance to make the issue right, the shop would much rather the matter was dealt with to everyones satisfaction then and there. If you don't feel like you're being taken seriously, ask to see a manager or supervisor and if you still aren't sure it's been taken onboard then follow up with an email before escalating it to head office or the over all owner.

Don't take the piss, we know when you're just chancing your arm to get something for free or a big discount. I've worked in more than one shop that had to ban some customers who complained about literally every purchase they made from us with the intention of getting it for next to nothing, and what they got was nothing.

I've mentioned it before but always be civil and reasonable, at least in the beginning, you'll get a lot more out of people that way.

Of course sometimes they are so incompetent, uncaring and infuriating that occasionally losing your rag is satisfaction enough when you know they aren't going to solve the issue and you are never going to purchase from them again.

In the interests of transparency I should say that I used to be an awful complainant to deal with, especially on issues of customer service. I tended to be overly forgiving of poor service in the initial stages of a transaction because I understood all of the factors we've spoken about previously. The only time it became an issue was when I realised that the sales person was just dicking me about. It's like a little switch flicks and the light comes on to show me that oh, you're just being casually shit on purpose because you think you can, or can't be arsed or you find it amusing?

This is when I would relax into it, now we know where we are. Out comes the passive aggression, condescension, getting someone to repeat what they've just said in a few different ways, asking for information about warranties and then just gazing off across their shoulder, asking about easy payment terms on £12 headphones until they were worn down or I was happy, whichever came first.

I'm not like that now of course, I think it was my hormones.

Speaking of which...

CHAPTER 10

PSYCHO TILLER

L ike all professions, retail can be very stressful and over the years I have found that the majority of my colleagues would deal with this in very traditional ways, such as -

Alcohol abuse

Recreational drugs

Nicotine

Crying

Sex (with or without anyone else)

Bottling it all up until it destroys your relationships at which point you can start crossing off the above methods on the list.

I have tried all of these with varying degrees of success. Alcohol abuse and nicotine to what I would estimate were Commonwealth Games standards. Crying and Sex to a very poor level, like the same level that kids at primary school who are playing football on a pitch in teams for the first time and you watch them and they all just run after the ball mindlessly in a massive group and have no idea where they are kicking it. That kind of level.

185

One of the ways I've dealt with work stress and anxiety is with terrible sleep patterns which have led to incredibly vivid and dangerous dreams. "Dangerous Dreams" sounds like the title of film Channel 5 might put on late at night for the Dad's who seemingly have no access to Internet pornography.

I have three dogs, one of which is a small black pug who has only one eye and, because his teeth never fully grew, a tongue that permanently hangs limp out of the side of his mouth (the side his remaining eye is on, which does make half his face look rather busy). In one particularly stressful period of work when I needed to somehow increase the customer numbers through a marketing campaign with no budget I had a particularly lucid dream that me and the pug were a tennis doubles team. I had no illusions as to my role in the partnership, I was

186

there merely as the requisite alternate returner/ receiver, like those moments when you see that Serena Williams is feeling a bit rusty so she puts herself into the doubles as well and you know she must have played with someone else but you've know idea who or what they even looked like. He was the star and what a star! He would hit his strokes holding the racket between his paws, standing on his back legs, before transferring it to his mouth whilst he scampered across court for the next return. He was really good, not winning a major good but definitely reaching quarters and semis of ranking tournaments quality, and it was at one of these indoor tournaments that we were about to play in the dream. One of those tournaments that I see inexplicably on Eurosport 2 or Amazon Prime TV on a Wednesday afternoon, with players you've never seen before in an event sponsored by Turkey's biggest mobile phone company and I always think that I must be one of only 12 people in the world watching it so how does it make money? Anyway, me and the pug are in the Netherlands for this evening indoor match and we are already at our end in our sponsored tracksuits warming up when the lights go down and the announcer goes into some enormous build up before smoke cannons go off and the two, dusty haired, athletic Dutch 20 year olds come out to rapturous home support. There are lights, chants, more smoke cannons, these two are really whipping up the crowd! I suddenly became absolutely incensed by this.

"Look at those pair of pricks! Fucking time wasting when we've warmed up! We'll have to go through it all again, it's a deliberate piss taking ploy!"

It's as I'm voicing my disgust to my pug partner (who incidentally seems entirely unmoved by the whole thing, I wish I had his focus) when they get out a four foot gold helium tennis ball from the crowd and start kicking around to each other. This is the last straw (or string) for me and I run over to the pair from Holland, my eyes focussed on the giant helium tennis ball which I am going to launch into the crowd with an enormous right footed kick and then we can get on to the match we're all here to play. I reach the ball and plant my standing foot to it's left, a perfect base for my right to swing through with power and precision, in the same manner as Jonny Wilkinson or Gareth Bale or a Moulin Rouge dancer. A beautiful back lift was converted to a powerful kick which not only saw the tennis ball soar into the crowd it also saw me, in the very real conscious world, launched from the side of my bed and headfirst into the corner of the bedside cabinet where it gashed my head open.

I sat myself up from my prone position, gently probed my bloodied head wound and wondered, if things had gone terribly wrong and I had become paralysed through this incident, would I tell anybody how it happened?   In later idle moments of reflection I also ponder whether there was an alternate universe where we really did meet on that tennis court and the pug and dutch contingent watched on in shock as the large Yorkshireman kicked the gold balloon and promptly disappeared. I also found out just how quickly someones sympathy evaporates into mocking laughter when they find out the reason for your injuries (wife/work colleagues).

My restless, broken sleep patterns continue, though now tennisless. If I could be bothered to learn the ins and outs of hydroponics, roof insulation and hacking into next doors electricity supply I think this would have been less of an issue.

There are a huge number of things in retail that can lead to stress, too many unsociable hours, worry of not receiving a living wage, balancing two part time jobs, falling figures, lack of footfall in the shops, they've still not sorted that fucking vending machine...the list goes on. I think retail as a whole has moved forward in regards to peoples mental health, especially from when I started when it wasn't even considered a recognised, valid issue. It still has a huge way to go there is still a big gap in the balance between work and home life for thousands of people which obviously leads to stress and illness and poorer productivity. Just to add to all this is the fact we are working in an essentially dying industry. Retail as it was before the pandemic does not exist any more. The supply chains are different, the move to online has grown exponentially and moving the country to an enormous trial of "Can we happily survive through just online shopping with a few beauticians, grocers and barbers on the high street?" The pandemic wasn't the cause, it just accelerated the main drivers of change. I certainly don't want to see the high street turned into some chain of Jorvik centre franchises where future generations will look on in wonder at these odd historic "shops" and ask "Why did they smell funny?"

It could indeed be an incredibly exciting time for shops, time for a clean slate and in the last part of this book I'm going to tell you what I would do with physical shopping because of my cleverness.

CHAPTER 11

TELL ME SOMETHING I DON'T KNOW

It's pretty obvious to everyone that barring an unforeseen successful luddite revolution we will not return to pre-pandemic styles of shopping. We've already seen the victors emerge from the Space To Let rubble and PPE landfill - Hair & Beauty, Food & Drink, Ant & Dec. In its current form there's probably only a generation left who rely on traditional shops for all their purchases and that market gets smaller every day.

So, where do we go from here? From a boring financial point of view a lot of what can happen relies on landlords being realistic in what their property is now worth in this new landscape. For all my retail career there was a constant emphasis on out performing the previous years figures. There was always a lot of chat along the lines of "Last year we were up 5% on the previous year so we're looking for a 5% increase on that", but far less conversation about how that was going to happen and everyone is always reticent to pop their hand up and say "...and how are we going to do that then?" For fear of being seen as negative. There's always an attitude from senior management that if you achieved it last year you must be able to do it again this year but better, because there's no way you all worked at your maximum last year. It's odd because I never saw them working 5% harder or better at any point. I'm assuming that they didn't all sit themselves down in the boardroom and say "Look, I had a cracking year last year but I know there's some previously untapped potential in me to be a 5% better manager than that this year and seemingly every subsequent year until I retire having achieved some superhuman level of retail excellence."

It sounds ridiculous because it is. You'd be astonished at how naive and inept seemingly successful large organisations are. Or maybe you wouldn't, given the number of businesses that have a "surprise" collapse after the real financials are revealed and the figures they've been massaging to give the impression of a never ending climbing success turns out to be years of losses. When the Bernie Madoff case was exposed I'm sure most people outside of his list of investors probably thought "Well of course it was a Ponzi scheme! How did they think he could keep on making huge profits every year?" and yet that same train of thought never extends to retailers. The assumption is that these juggernauts of shopping will march on relentlessly upwards.

I worked for a number of large retailers who (at least at store level) didn't keep a diary or record of the year so when they had to look at how to improve in the upcoming year or why messenger bags were up 200% in June and July they had to rely on the memory of the people who'd been there. Maybe there'd been a promotion, maybe they'd been featured on a popular TV programme, could have been that viral thing on TikTok, they'd never know, and if they couldn't learn from the past they're already on the back-foot planning for success in the future. There was always a kind of laissez faire attitude that if that if the business planned on an increase then there must be one coming along and if it didn't and the shop closed then, at that time in terms of the actual physical retail spaces being made or available it didn't used to really matter.

Businesses would come and go, shops would close and open with another sign above the door more successful than the last. If you wanted a guaranteed source of ever increasing income, become a retail landlord, preferably with your base offshore so you don't have to contribute to the upkeep of the society you profit from. In the not too distant past these landlords could sign up large retailers to 20, sometimes 25 year leases and much like high level football managers it didn't matter if the whole thing went tits up because you'd still get your payout and another club/retailer would be along in a month with more money and blind optimism that this time, this time it would work. This success could never end, that's why pension investors threw large amounts of other peoples futures at these retail real estate holders. As long as people wanted to leave their homes to go purchase items then this business model cannot fail. As online grew, landlords realised that retailers weren't quite so enthusiastic about banking on a quarter of a centuries future success and so they took a ten year lease offer and now you can twist their arm for a five year term if you chuck in a staff discount card. Even without the previous never ending revenue stream of new store openings these landlords are still clinging onto the old model. We often see in the news about retailers negotiating with landlords and that's because the retailers are existing in the current timeline whilst the landlords are seemingly still writing on parchment and pelting peasants with turnips, happy enough to see stores empty with no income rather than full with a more realistic turnover. Quite where they think they are going to get retailers to fill these units at old rates and with investors moving their money elsewhere I have no idea and frankly I could not give less of a shit. When you are dealing with people who think the answer to lower incomes from retail parks is not to introduce better facilities to encourage people to visit more but to install cameras to fine visitors for being parked there too long it becomes clear the kind of arseholes you are dealing with.

Anyway, enough of the negative, let's be 5% more positive and look at where we can go from here.

A LITTLE PICK ME UP

"Pick up points" or "Click & Collect" are still an untapped source of potential and will be until we're all working from home or have some unfeasibly large and secure drop off box outside our houses (good luck in a flat). Right now they are tagged on to existing businesses and always feel like an after thought but there is real potential for small independents to build this into their business model right from the start.

Not sure if your locally sourced craft ale and artisanal bar snacks idea can support a retail space on it's own throughout the year? Maybe it could with a dedicated pick up point built in, if I'm picking up a parcel after work I would definitely be treating myself to a few bottles of "Old Rusty Weed Whacker" and a packet of "Carol's Cow Crunch", why not, I've deserved it. I'm currently less inclined to make a spontaneous purchase at my current pick up point - the local chemist. In my dream scenario these small local pick up points become modern day versions of the romantic Irish pubs that serve stout on one side of the bar and fix your bicycle on the other. Large chains haven't really got to grips with the potential of pick up opportunities, preferring instead to either make the experience of finding out where to go and what to do akin to solving an "Only Connect" puzzle by braille or make it so easy to ignore any other shopping opportunities in the service that they effectively do themselves out of a sale. I'm sure there is a logic by having a dedicated collection point at a separate entrance so customers don't have to enter the retail environment you spend thousands on creating, I just can't see it right now, just like your produce.

SPIN ME RIGHT ROUND BABY

I've spent years moving shopfit and fixtures around shop floors and at every point I've said "Why don't they put fucking wheels on these?" It's obviously because way back when the likes of Mr Selfridge and young Johnny Lewis were filling out their orders they were under the assumption that once these fixtures were inside the shop they wouldn't be moving until they fell apart. This tradition has been carried by people who have never worked in a shop for decades "Why would I make these mobile? My glorious idea is everlasting?" I say all this, not because I am part of a "Big-Wheel" agenda or because I am tired of lifting things but because making your fixtures mobile creates a huge amount of flexibility, not only in terms of the layout opportunities but in how your retail space is used. A vast amount of shops still have the architecture from when large storage space was needed, now that most retailers get their stock replenishment when it's needed these "back of house" storage spaces can be used for other functions. Having the ability to both move and remove fixtures lets you recreate what the space can be used for. Maybe teaching and classes, I'm sure that there'd be a few takers on a "John Lewis Fine Arts Diploma". You could hold a table tennis league, chess school, film club, host acoustic live bands, find something that relates to your brand. The rent for the floor space doesn't stop once the doors are closed so why not carry on using it after you traditionally stop trading? Even if all you do just helps the community and builds relationships in the long run you never know when you need those same people. Besides all that I've never understood the fixation with things staying the same, your spare bedroom can double as your office, your dining table can host Warhammer, I'm pretty sure your furniture shop could host Book Club on a Wednesday night and sell coffee and cake at the same time.

ARE YOU EXPERIENCED?

Creating an "experience" for customers has been something for Jessica and Jamie to bring up as an aim for them whenever the meeting happens to discuss what they're going to bring to the company next year. It's a wonderfully vague yet exciting phrase that hints at both being new, profitable and at the same time entirely unmeasurable as a concept. It could be anything from daylight bulbs in the fitting rooms to elephant birthing on the second floor. It also means you can trot out any old toss when it comes to deciding whether it was a success or not. Elephant birthing? Massive on social media. Daylight bulbs in the fitting room? Great customer feedback on Trust Pilot. Coming up with concepts without deciding on a measure of success is a perfect way for some people to do half a job and is a big old pile of wank. It's not hard - did more people come into the shop because of what you did, did you sell more?

Shops are pretty boring right now, people aren't necessarily looking for sword swallower angle grinding a metal codpiece to help them find the perfect sauté pan but in an age where it takes longer to choose what to watch on Netflix than it does to watch the programme they do want some stimulation. "Experience" in retail should be not only how you feel in the shop and how you feel after leaving but also how you feel about the shop much later. We're still in an age of chain stores wanting everyone to have the same experience in every shop they have, regardless of customer types or location. For some reason retailers want you to think that you could be in one of their shops anywhere in the world and it would look the same. This shows an incredible amount of self confidence in the environment you're creating to imagine that someone might think "I know I'm in the Istanbul branch of Burton's but now I'm inside I could be in the the one in Pontefract!" as if that's a good thing.

Smaller independent suppliers have had to look at emphasising the provenance as a selling feature, "We are like this because of where we are."   Large chains are essentially saying "Nothing here has any worth, have this and be happy about it."   Generations of character is dismissed in the planning, when in reality people might want your infrastructure, buying power, fashion sense but they don't necessarily want to feel like everywhere is anywhere. Cities and towns have their own identities and these should be celebrated and reflected in the shops there. This is often done in so called "Flagship" shops, usually in London, usually near head office, usually the only shops that get visited on a regular basis by people who sign off on the finances. They are also the shops that have the least relevance to the rest of the country, especially the ones on Oxford Street where a large proportion of the customers are transient tourists where the effort of making a difference from the rest of the chain is largely lost.

I worked for a chain that regularly put the same old box into any town but when the time came for putting one in the bosses home city then we had a different beauty hall, different mannequins, references to the city were everywhere in artworks and sculpture, the location was celebrated throughout and you could tell what city you were in even when you were inside and the stock was largely the same. It didn't take much more money, just an interest and a passion for the location. Endless stores are planned, built and opened without the person buying or creating the interior ever having visited the location, most of the time the don't even google image the place, just another shop to consult on the spreadsheet. Customers don't have to visit any more, you need to make them want to and palming them off with cookie cutter builds isn't good enough any more. In larger chains this is often because the decision makers have become too distant from the objective. I'm not saying they need to work part time in a shop, visits to the actual physical locations where your customers make decisions on investing in what you have seems to a lot of the decision makers to be a waste of time.

I used to love looking at the layouts of shops to see what would be the most enjoyable and helpful route for customers. What they see at various points as they make their way around. Making sure the lighting was focused in the right way to emphasise the product. It was like curating an exhibition and yet when we would receive visits from head office decision makers it always felt like it was a chore for them. Well mate, if you're fucking bored how do you expect the customers to feel, how do you expect the staff to feel?

Populating your retail management structure with people who have no interest in shopping has always baffled me. How do businesses achieve any degree of long lasting success when the people steering the ship have no interest in the core service they provide? Well, they don't any more. Their previous virtual monopoly has gone with the growth and eventual, inevitable dominance of internet retail. Now anyone can be a retailer, in some cases you won't need to hold any stock. You certainly don't need to pay a ridiculous rent and rates fee for a physical location. Now all of a sudden the questions for the managers of physical estates become that bit harder. In my time on the shop floor it was not unusual to have a visit from a regional manager or someone from head office and they would spend a third of the time walking the shop floor, a third of the time "back of house" looking at stockrooms etc and a third in the office talking to the various levels of management in the store. So two thirds of their time was looking at elements that didn't take any money and that the customer didn't see. Obviously these things still need looking at but they are both there purely to facilitate taking money on the shop floor so why spend two thirds of your time on something that earns you nothing?

There is, as in most businesses, a ridiculous amount of politicking, so whenever there was a visit you would find ambitious managers clambering over each other to get themselves known to the visiting deity. Seemingly, it turns out, nobody wanted to be doing the job they had, or if they did want their current role, they wanted it to be somewhere else, preferably bigger and more boast-worthy. This obviously has plus points with a lot of driven, promotion hungry and ambitious staff members. It also leads to an inordinate amount of back scratching sycophants who focus on achieving certain key things, whether they're relevant to taking money or not so that they can be noticed enough to make that move from supervisor to assistant manager, then department manager, deputy manager, store manager, regional manager and then on to any number of bullshit monikers in the head office managerial labyrinth. For a group of people who've spent a lot of time extolling the virtues of their shops they certainly can't seem to wait to get away and never see them again.

"What the hell has this got to do with anything?" You might quite rightly ask. Well, with online commerce becoming the dominant force in retail a rather disillusioned physical shop chicken has come home to roost only to find that the coop hasn't been maintained in the last 20 years (for the sake of my metaphor I'm going to ignore the average lifespan of a laying hen). Despite these business leading visionaries seeing people largely as an annoyance in the spreadsheet, these same people put virtually no effort into their online presence. They don't try to hide what they think of you as an employee, it's in the title they give to the department that deals with you - "Human Resources", you're a thing like transport or warehousing or fuel.

INTERMISSION

At this point it's probably worth me explaining the rather rambling nature of the last section.

At time of writing this my mum has just recently died. This is my first bit of work since the funeral, well apart from the eulogy.

So far this year I've lost my job and had my remaining parent die and there is still time left for me to move house and complete a line on the "stressful things to happen" bingo. To bring this to a related note, my mother hated shopping and shops. Even though there was a small supermarket at the end of her road she still wouldn't visit, using instead my sister as a proto Ocado delivery service, placing her order with her when she came on her daily visits. Going to the shops would have cut down on her TV watching time which consisted of her absorbing the world through the full gamut of what was available from the lit box. She was like David Bowie in "The Man Who Fell To Earth" if he hadn't come from space but from Goole instead. We once took her to Ikea where she reached the furniture department and dropped onto a sofa exclaiming "Leave me here" in the dramatic fashion of one of those Vietnam war films from the 1980's except instead of being airlifted out by a Huey helicopter amongst grenade smoke and gunfire we popped over to the dining table section and went back to get her before the flat pack bit at the end (or "Saigon" as it is now referred to by us). Unlike the Americans, my mother had learnt from her history and knew full well that she shouldn't be there, it wasn't for her.

Now, where were we?

Ah, yes...

ARE YOU A BIT MORE EXPERIENCED?

Here are a few more simple little tips for shopkeepers large and small.

R etailers would do well to take notes and inspiration from the best art installations. These are pure passive experience, created solely to instil an emotion in the visitor through creating something new and unexpected within a traditional architectural space. Instead of consulting traditional retail designers it is now time bring in the creators of art installations, set designers, film concept artists. Making your own stores playlist to give your shop a brand identity and atmosphere is one thing but why not commission your own bespoke soundtrack? Your "Lo Fi HipHop Beats To Shop To" playlist might be a nice background but it's easily replicated elsewhere. Commission your own work and not only will it be unique to you but marketing who you've commissioned the work from can be used in your news and social media.

Every new collection whether it be clothes, furniture or bathroom accessories has been designed with inspiration and a theme in mind, so why not let me in on the process? If you came up with a range of pans after imagining what Marcello Mastroianni would have in his kitchen, tell me that and show me it in mood boards, pictures, artefacts, build his imaginary kitchen and merchandise the product on it. All these designs come from effort and imagination so why hide such an interesting part of that from me?

Shop lighting is at best functional. Lighting is an incredibly powerful mood creator and yet it is treated as an afterthought in so many instances. We are in a time when homeowners can control the colour and luminescence of every bulb in their house from their phone and yet the high street has been content with general cover lighting with a few spotlights to add the glamour. Why light your evening wear in the same way as your kitchenware? Get a lighting designer in at the start so that you both know what the purpose and mood of each area should be and make the lighting rig flexible so you aren't stuck when flexing your space in different seasons. Oh, and I shouldn't have to say this to multi million pound retailers but - make sure your bulbs are lit and clean you fucking peasants.

Understanding your products. Both Apple and their consumer devotees get (in some instances rightly) ridiculed.

The company has always come across as pious in its slavish devotion to design, which often loses its balance over the line from aesthetically pleasing to impractical. "You want to be able to plug in your headphones? No, my simple minded friend, the hole it needs is an abomination to the lines I have created on this phone, no you must purchase bluetooth headphones. You want multiple ports on your laptop and have them easily accessible? Out vile peasant! You shall have HALF the number of ports you require! This is not some mere piece of ephemeral electronic fluff you are purchasing here, this is design, visceral, red in tooth and claw. Its seamless aluminium case leaving you both in awe and humbled in its genius. Until next years version comes out. And whilst you are here may I remind you it is a MACBOOK that should sit astride a reclaimed wood dining table lit by vintage bulbs to be used for writing books on equality or designing electric carts for disabled dogs, not some common *"laptop"* smeared, no doubt, with the detritus of your pornographic consumption." Some cynical people might suggest that they deliberately hold back features and technology to better drip feed it out in selling yearly model updates, but that's not me. The one thing you can't accuse of Apple though is not being obsessed with itself and it's products. This is taken all the way through to its packaging where it gives the impression that a team of people have slaved over the design decisions involved in a small white cardboard box for months. Their annual pronouncements and ads urging the followers to keep the date so that we may all sit amongst the virtual congregation to hear the latest chip news.

"Look mate, loads of companies do the same thing. It's not like Samsung are knocking out Galaxy's in a shed and drawing the box in biro" you might well say and you'd be right. The difference is that Apple so obviously loves what they make and wants, nay expects, you to do the same that it is infectious. You just don't get that same impression with other electronics brands. Partially because they are usually incredibly diverse in what they produce. Oh what, you love the new phone you've brought out? Well I was here yesterday and you said the same thing about a crane you made and I'm booked in a week on Thursday to hear you tell me what a revelation this new van you've built is. If you want people to come to you specifically for what you sell and how you sell it, at some point you have to draw a line in the sand to say "This is who we are" and run with it. As an example, as a fairly average consumer of electronics I would find it pretty much impossible to tell what the difference is between similarly specced laptops from HP, Acer, Asus, Dell and Lenovo is. I do know that you don't find them next to Apple products that do essentially the same tasks in shops or on websites. They are gathered, huddled together in the anonymous "other" category.

L et's say there was another machine there but it's not all round edged, thin and dark. It's boxy, bright orange. In place of touch sensitive functions there are physical clicks switches and buttons and because it's not trying to be as diaphanous as an angels wing. It's got room for a battery that lasts a reasonable length of time and there's space at the side for all the different ports you want. Maybe it would be made by a company like Teenage Engineering who produce some incredible pieces of music technology, perhaps they'd aim it at music makers? Someone with the confidence to say they love what they make and think you will too. I would definitely be interested. But then it was my idea.

Edit: This sort of now exists since I first wrote this with Teenage engineering now making an orange PC case.

What I'm floundering around to say is love what you sell and if you don't love it but you think it would sell, put it under another brand name, cherish what you stand for and that infection will rub off. Just do it in the right way, not like smoothie makers who I always imagine have weddings that look like the set of Midsommar.

When it comes to people, it shouldn't need saying but look after your staff. You don't have to give them all a company car and a couple of lines of coke every Friday afternoon. Pay them a reasonable wage for their efforts, include them in conversation about the direction the business is taking. Be honest. Be kind. Have some empathy and understanding for their personal circumstances and they will repay it in effort and loyalty. It's not hard or complicated, just don't be a dick. The other thing I will mention though is if you do manage to achieve all these aims, don't bang on about it as if it's worthy of a marketing campaign, it's basic human dignity. There was a certain manufacturer of products that liked to portray themselves as less of a company and more a gang of great mates who all loved each other and loved what they did. A fun product made by friends, just like you and me. Only later it turns out that they weren't just like you and me because a large amount of their previous employees came out to say that there had been a history of systemic bullying and favouritism that had led them to leave and find work somewhere else. Oh dear, less "Friends - the sitcom" and more "Scum - the film". This hasn't held them back though, in their most recent ad the seem to be suggesting that they are both a part of the front line in reducing climate change and a leading exponent of inclusivity (although admittedly they only mention their customers, not employees). This hasn't changed my view on them or my purchasing decisions because I'd always had a suspicion that they were a bunch of arseholes anyway but it has affected other peoples and their marketing now comes across as saying "You might have heard some horrible things about how we treat people, but it's not all people and look! Over there! We're planting some trees!"

Planting trees seems to be the Climate Catholics confession and Hail Mary. It's a nice easy thing for us plebeians to get our head round when it comes to the temperature carnage around us but I think at some point we're going to have to face the fact that it's not a tree shortage that's got us in this mess so planting them is not going to get us out of it. It's a clever sleight of hand for companies to talk about being "carbon neutral" and tree planting when they are essentially saying "I'm going to carry on just as I was before but if I give you some money for some trees somewhere will you stop hassling us about making expensive changes to our work practices?" and all the while people at home are being told to try not to make unnecessary car journeys and the electric bulbs we'd previously been told to turn off when not in use are now still killing the planet and we need to put them all in landfill and buy new ones that cost £8 not 57p. If people thought of themselves as businesses they would be saying "New bulbs? That's an unexpected expense. How about I plant a couple of trees (or say I have) and claim back that £7.43 from a "Green Tax"? Come to think of it have another couple of saplings and I'll start heating the house by burning all of my recycling in a metal bin in the garden".

A large internet company that specialised in helping people find things on the net used to have a motto of "Don't be evil". Admirable stuff, until they stopped using it, which does then leave you with the impression that they're saying "Look guys, we gave it a go. It was a nice idea, it really was but we've realised that when push comes to shove we are both willing and able to be real cunts to get more money. It was a nice thought though, you've got to give us that."

Anyway, as I said, look after your staff.

Take the lead. The bigger the company the slower they are to make different or interesting decisions, they get safe and they get stale waiting for someone else to take the risk so they can follow or step back. It's people being brave and taking a risk that got these businesses formed in the first place. Your finance teams are there to be the Golden Hour on Radio 2 and you should be John Peel [*note to myself - make sure to ask a young person for the current equivalents of these - don't want to show my age*].   Stay clear of old hackneyed retailing. The eagle eyed and dolphin brained amongst you will have spotted that the large starting capital letters in this section come together to spell **RESULT** and it's exactly this tawdry old shit you need to avoid to keep the people you work with engaged. We've all sat in training rooms where these things are trotted out and immediately forgotten not only the message from each letter but the word they spelled "Was it RESTARTS? No, RECOUNTS...REFUNDS?" If you absolutely must do it use words that will be memorable - VAGINA, BALLBAG, FANNY, BELLEND.   That kind of thing, don't feel restricted, let your mind go.

Not that you would notice from your experience in most high street retailers but the primary message their staff are battered around the head with is that old trope of the customer coming first. "Without them, where would we be?" They ask, presumably rhetorically, in induction training. Well, that alternate reality has come to visit over the last couple of years. The customer coming first over the other tasks that you have to do working in a shop is rarely prioritised unless the shop has a "Visit" as we've previously talked about. We've all had that experience when you need help from a staff member and felt like you were an unnecessary distraction from the real work of opening cardboard boxes while on their knees. It's tempting at this point to think that your sales assistant isn't treating you with the requisite attention, and you'd be right, it's just that the waters have already been muddied that day by the "customer comes first" message being slightly made slightly opaque by the subsequent message of "Get those boxes out onto the shelves before 11, no breaks until then." So then you're now dealing with someone on minimum wage who hasn't eaten or drank anything for five and a half hours, doing soulless manual work and now you're expecting to be cap doffed through the aisles to those storage boxes "Mrs Hinch" uses on Instagram. It's not necessarily the assistants fault they come off as brusque and uninterested, it's just not been prioritised by the person who gives them permission to take on fluids. Having said that you will undoubtedly come across a vast array of fucking useless pricks who work in shops. I know, I've have worked with them, hired some and ,on occasion, been one.

It's one of those principals that absolutely needs to be adhered to for a great customer experience but also needs a degree of common sense and a sense of team work and common goals from all involved. If you see your team mate has been helping a customer for an extended period of time and haven't been able to get all of their stock out it's then you need to drop in and help out until they get back. That way you can all get the job done on time, the customer's happy and you can both go on your break to slag off that lazy toss of a manger who should have been overseeing that kind of thing anyway if they hadn't been too hungover/depressed/busy chasing that new starter for a potential shag.

CHAPTER 12

CLOSING TIME & CASHING UP

It's time for us to lock those doors, cash up the tills, stick the money in the safe, get our coats and go. If you work in a 24 hour operation it's time to welcome in the Mole People who will take over for the evening. Lovely bunch but let's face it, they've got some pretty dark issues that it's probably best not to press them on at the pub. If you work in a shop with normal closing hours it's time to have some frankly revelatory gossip half relayed to you in the locker room by Anne (who by the way had fuck all to say all day and now she drops this bombshell?!) while you get your coat that you'll carry on on in the

231

WhatsApp group in an hour or two once everyone has got home and had a glass/smoke/swallow of whatever is their chosen relaxant.

If you are lucky enough to be granted "Key Holder" status it means you get to leave later than everyone else and stand in the rain at the back door whilst waiting for the alarm of the shop to set only for it to inevitably say there is a fault that means you have to go back in and check all the doors before finding that stockroom door ajar that Dave said he'd definitely closed before making a mental note to make sure he doesn't get a raise in his appraisal. All that for the prestige and an extra 10p an hour. Sometimes, if you're a Key Holder and you're really lucky you'll get a phone call at half two in the morning and have to go all the way back into work because some pissed up cock has broken a window on his way home because Andrea has never really loved him, she never really got over

Steve even though she always said she had. *Fucking Steve, I'd smash that little cunts face into this window if he was here. See this Andrea? Is this who you love really? This little shit?* And there goes the window. Foot on glass, and all of a sudden there's that sudden sharp depressing clarity. That water splash to the face, not so much ice cold, more tepid. That feeling that maybe it wasn't Steve's brilliance that was turning her head, maybe he just hadn't let himself go like you had, maybe he just made an effort. He wasn't any bigger or stronger. He wasn't brighter. His hair was always pretty cool though and, in fairness, he did make an effort with his clothes. *I've just taken my eye off the ball, I need to sort my shit out, knock the boozing on the head, pay her a bit more attention, I was a bit of a catch in my day, get in the gym. Yeah, I can turn this around!*

233

I think of this as I sit on the shop counter waiting for the glazier to come and fit some emergency perspex to the previously intact glass door at three in the morning. I hope Andrea and the pissed up cock make a go of it, I truly do, we've all been there. My feelings towards Steve are at best ambivalent. Sometimes in these moments you get to have a chat with which ever police people might be around at the time. I have had the odd interaction with the police but barring a stint in an identity parade and being caught speeding all my police interactions have been through my work in retail. This almost always included trying to find and identify a shoplifter or hanging round in the early hours waiting for glaziers. Sometimes I'd be in the office and a couple of male officers would come in to look at CCTV footage of a shoplifting regular and a sizeable amount of the hetero female population of the staff would suddenly turn into the ageing cast of a Carry On film, all "Phwoars" and "taking down my particulars". I'd feel a sense of new "right on" 80's disgust at their baseness until a couple of times a female pony tailed PC came to look at the footage and I understood it (*that tactical vest*).

So, we're at the end of the day and our chat. I know I've said it before but given the theme of the book I think it stands repeating, I love shops and can't imagine a future without them. There is going to be a bright and brilliant future for some and the people that work in them and for others this is a very definite full stop. I'm sad that, despite my inherent dislike of interacting with the general population, this is another erosion of that much needed part of our lives. I'm fine with the principle but I don't think we know what fulfils the gap it leaves just yet.

Shops can be glorious places, full of awe and excitement. They can be a bit shambolic and grown from the soil of the past. They can help you feel good for that date tonight. They can help you make that change from skinny to baggy. They can give you the only conversation you've had all day and not care if your voice sounds odd from such little use. They can show you how to wear that weird bag that is neither one thing nor another or just make you wonder if people anywhere really hang out together like the mannequins do in the Zara windows.

I'm sure a form of shop will emerge and flourish and we'll all look and laugh at how quaint everything seemed to be.

"Look! They're pushing a cart around and putting things in! When did they start following us around and selecting the items for us then Dad?"

Shops also shaped the architecture of our populated centres to a degree and even relatively recently there have been some wonderfully creative buildings made possible by retailing. It's not just the function to shop on the high street that we could lose. It's like the little coral reef of life that it supports, the delivery people, the bars that are helped to survive by the post work drinkers, the newsagent, those sandwich shops that are run on the money from shop workers, the window cleaners, the bin men, that jacket potato van that seems to have been there since Thatcher took over, the nice security guys who always let me into the precinct car park before they locked the main gate so I didn't have to walk all the way round after rushing to finish locking up on a late.

I think at this point it's become impossible for me to unpick the reality from the romanticism, the history from the memory, I've worked for too long in high street retailing to not have a certain pink tint to my glasses and to feel an unease about the changes that may come.

But now is not the time to worry, now is the time to get out there and see if Jason has got a frame for that print my wife hates, Jess has got those heated gloves in the bike shop so my hands don't freeze off this year and while I'm out it would be rude not to have mocha from the van by the statue, even though I'm only really going there to see his dog.

They might seem like just a background to our lives but one day that amber/cream light they cast on the pavement as you walk home in the rain may be gone for good and how will we all feel then?

ABOUT THE AUTHOR

Rich Scarr has spent over 30 years in retail.

Waitering in A-road food stops, manning customer service phone lines, managing decorating shops, serving on a hundred shop floors filled with childrenswear, womenswear, menswear through to window dressing and visual merchandising, he has done it all with vastly different levels of competency. Now he writes things down for you to read. You may also find him drawing things for you to look at.

Does having a podcast qualify as broadcasting? Almost certainly not but, for the purposes of this book I'm willing to stretch credulity and say "Writer and Broadcaster". He talks about various aspects of popular culture on the "Week Points" podcast.

He also still styles his shelves at home as if they were a window display which is a bit sad really (although he doesn't put price tickets on them, which is something).

ACKNOWLEDGEMENTS

I'd like to thank Lucy, Chris, Simone and Nick for reading this as I was finishing bits and have me say "Is it ok? Is it shit?" In a variety of ways. Your feedback and support was extremely appreciated.

I'd like to thank the amazing people I've had as work colleagues over the years, you genuinely kept me sane and still here, I think you know who you are.

On a similar note I'd also like to thank all the arses I've worked with as well for giving me some of the material for this book, I'm sure you know who you are.

Last but not least I'd like to Diane for supporting me through this venture, especially when I needed picking up and shaking from the funk I occasionally fell in.

I cannot thank her for reading the book though as she said it's "Not really her thing". When I asked her if she'd listen to the audiobook version I'm doing she still said no, when I asked why she said "because it's you isn't it? It would be weird". With that kind of feedback I'm surprised I didn't get this finished earlier.

Printed in Great Britain
by Amazon